An architectural guide
Carlo Scarpa

Sergio Los

Carlo Scarpa
An architectural guide

arsenale e† editrice

Sergio Los
CARLO SCARPA
AN ARCHITECTURAL GUIDE

Series editor
Sergio Polano

Design
Michela Scibilia

Translation
Antony Shugaar

Printed in Italy by
EBS Editoriale Bortolazzi-Stei
Verona

Reprint
November 2001

Arsenale Editrice
A division of EBS
via Monte Comun 40
37057 San Giovanni
Lupatoto (Vr)
www.arsenale.it

© Copyright 1995
Arsenale Editrice srl

ISBN 88-7743-145-8

Photographs
Sergio and Sofia Los

Photo credits
Amministrazione Provinciale of
Parma (file 14)
Archivio Fotografico Museo
Correr, Venice (files 10, 20)
ASAC – Archivio Storico delle
Arti Contemporanee, La Biennale
of Venice (file 9)
Marino Barovier, Venice (p. 14)
Alessandra Chemollo, Venice
(file 19)
Roberto Collovà, Palermo
(file 39)
Arch. Giuseppe Martelli, Genoa
(file 41)
Studio fotografico Maria Ida Biggi,
Venice (file 22)
Studio fotografico Mark E. Smith,
Venice (files 19, 29)
Victory Interactive Media SA,
Lugano (file 27)
Italo Zannier, Venice (file 29)

The publisher wishes to express his
thanks to the Photo Archive of the
Soprintendenza ai Beni Artistici
e Storici of Venice for having kindly
authorised the publication of pictures
of file 3.

Contents

To Carlo Scarpa

The architecture of Carlo Scarpa, which the reader is about to survey, is introduced in this guide in two separate sections. The first section tells the reader just who Scarpa is, describes the origins of his architecture, and outlines the design experimentation in which his architecture was involved; the second section, which accompanies the illustrations, is meant to serve as a guide for use in surveying that architecture, inviting the reader to take particular note of certain architectural events and indicating the features that distinguish, in the author's view, Scarpa's architecture. This guide, of course, is not meant to supply a rigorous, thorough-going interpretation of Scarpa's work; it is meant rather to help the reader — who may not yet have looked into the subject — to understand; as well as to encourage the reader to study the subject in greater depth.

1 — A textual architecture

In order to provide an introduction to the design process and accompanying research activity of Carlo Scarpa, in a manner appropriate to his thought and to his work, I would like to suggest to the reader a "textual" approach. The buildings, therefore, should be examined as if they narrated a number of stories: stories about everyday living — the houses — and stories about works of art — the museums. To adopt this approach further means that we will always consider two aspects of Scarpa's work, one aspect that concerns their content, i.e., the stories that the works tell; and a second aspect that has to do with the mode of expression, the way in which these stories are told. If we wish to interpret the works of Scarpa as if they were so many texts, then we shall have to begin by examining the way in which his architectural "language" operates. In order to avoid the confusion that is so typical of semiotics, dominated as it is by the study of verbal languages, I shall refer to this rather different language as an architectural "symbolic system" (or, to put it more concisely, "architectural system," or even "compositional system"). Let me specify only that, despite the many points of similarity with word-based language, the organization of the "architectural system" differs radically from that of literary forms of expression. The two aspects that are indicated above become, in architecture, the "typological content" and the "compositional system": the former constitutes the "story" that the building will tell, while the latter represents the "discourse," i.e., the method of telling that story.

2 — The Sculpture Gallery of Canova, a critical design

Anyone who visits the Gipsoteca, or Sculpture Gallery, in Possagno, for instance, quickly realizes that it recounts the sculptures of Canova by placing them in a certain light: that special diaphanous light which allows one to view the statues becomes, for Scarpa, a remarkable tool of architectural critique, far more effective than the verbal tools that are used by art critics. It is precisely that remarkable light, which reveals the illuminated sculptures and which "traduces" Canova by offering a new interpretation, that constitutes the typological content of the museum — along with the organization of the rooms and the construction as a whole, of course. Scarpa "opens a discourse" concerning this content by means of a specific "compositional system," distinguished by the use of specific figurative elements, ranging from the trihedrons of the openings — which produce that remarkable, specific light — to the steps that accompany the visitor throughout the tour, from the materials used all the way to the arrangement that gives the sculptures life, as if they were persons themselves.

The rooms, which are the basic propositions of architecture, make literal those metaphors used so frequently in literary criticism when explaining artworks with such terms as "to show" or to "cast light upon" some aspect or other. I first saw Canova's statues back in the Fifties, before Scarpa designed and built the installation that now houses them; to see them in the new Sculpture Gallery was a revelation. The architect makes room for the sculptures and places them in the correct light, in such a way that they "constitute" the space which they occupy; it would now be inconceivable to remove them or to shift them. This "creating space in the light"[1] illuminates the works while revealing their meaning. It seems to me that in this architecture one can clearly comprehend the statement that "the essential nature of a work of art

is equally shared by those who create it and by those who safeguard it. It is, however, the work itself that makes possible those who create it, and that demands, in terms of its own essential existence, those who safeguard it. The fact that art lies at the origin of the creation means that art points to the essential existence of those who are coessential to it: the creators and the safeguarders."[2] Therefore, in the opinion of Heidegger, Canova and Scarpa are equally essential to the fundamental nature, as works of art, of the sculptures which are displayed in the Sculpture Gallery.

I would like to consider architecture as an art that "distinguishes" a place; Scarpa distinguishes the place in question with light and with luminous space, which are in this case the components making up the Sculpture Gallery. The "distinctive" qualities of the architecture become a cognitive tool, used to understand and to help to understand the sculptures of Canova, in the case of Possagno, and many other works, in the several installations that make up the work of Carlo Scarpa. The subject — or content — of the explorations of the world of design of Carlo Scarpa, therefore, can be considered to be more the sculpture of Canova than the building that houses those sculptures, as if Scarpa had been asked to write/build an architectural essay on the statues in question. Even though in Scarpa's text, because it is poetic, the "discourse," (i.e., the way in which the essay or sculpture gallery is organized) is every bit as important as the "story" that it tells (meaning the sculptures that constitute its content), it seems fundamental to me to single out the distinction between examining this architecture as

9

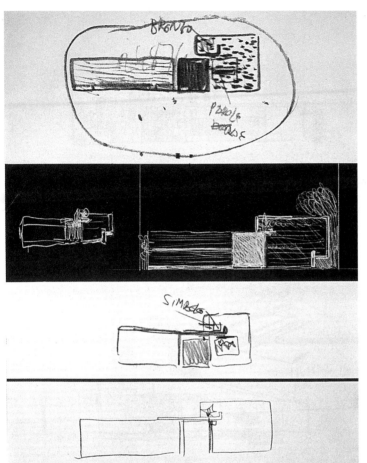

4.
Carlo Scarpa,
*Drawings from the plan
for the entrance to the
IUAV*, Venice, 1966;
the drawings are
reproduced from the
book by Sergio Los,
*Carlo Scarpa architetto
e poeta*, Cluva, Venice,
1967.

a "text" and using it as a "tool." As a "text" the Sculpture
Gallery can express a certain content, it can exemplify a type and
its various properties; as a "tool" — a sort of "machine à exposer,"
or displaying machine — it could do no more than to function,
perhaps by entertaining the visitors with its own mute loveliness.
The felicitous approach that Scarpa has taken with respect to those
sculptures has been that of sharing his experience with the visitor: the building endows the works with a significance that adds
to their value, making them more desirable. The work that
Scarpa has done on the subject of the sculptures by Canova, using architecture as a language of critique, seems quite similar to
the working method that Walter Benjamin made his own, developing the Romantic concept of criticism: a method that strives
to attain a completion of the work, rather than a judgement. In
Scarpa's work, just as in Benjamin's work, "criticism is an ex-
periment performed upon a work of art, in which reflection is
aroused, through that reflection, the work of art is elevated to an

awareness and knowledge of itself."[3] In this sense, I have claimed that the architecture of Carlo Scarpa works as a symbolic system — as an architectural language — and that once it has become a "language" it becomes the "means" by which one can conceive/produce a reality rather than being the "subject" of conception/production. It seems worthwhile to me to place considerable emphasis upon this reversal of design process with respect to the functionalist ideology according to which, on the contrary, work is what research sets out to examine.[4] The hermeneutic approach of Scarpa's architecture explains its critical capacity; it makes easily understandable his commitment to using architecture in displaying works of art that is so characteristic of much of his work.

3 — Compositional system and typological content

When Carlo Scarpa received the Premio Olivetti for architecture and town planning, in 1956, he shared it with Ludovico Quaroni. In assigning these two prizes, the commission intended to indicate its approbation of Quaroni's commitment to the typological content of architecture and Scarpa's work in the context of his compositional system. We shall briefly consider these two aspects of Scarpa's architectural design approach, which I have previously introduced.

As far as the "typological content" is concerned, the central issue addressed by Scarpa was the installation of museums, exhibitions, and so on; it is, in short, the art of displaying a figurative text, and it included the restoration of existing buildings, new architecture,

11

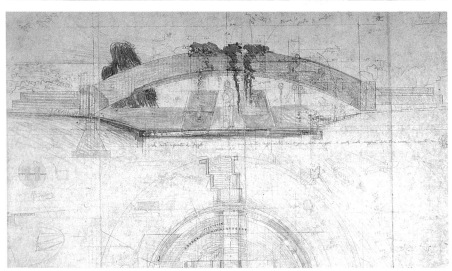

12

7.
Katsushika Hokusai,
Bridge, Tokyo, 1827-
1830, Gutenberg
Museum, Mainz.

8.
Carlo Scarpa, *Querini
Stampalia Foundation*,
Venice, 1961-1963;
the bridge that leads
to the entrance.

9.
Carlo Scarpa, *Brion
Family Monumental
Tomb*, San Vito
d'Altivole (Treviso),
1969-1976; the
Archisolium.

as well as ancient, old, and contemporary works of art. Scarpa's design work, however, made no distinction between the display of artworks inside of the buildings and the display of the buildings themselves. His rehabilitation design made the monument eloquent, just as his installations made the works on display eloquent. When Scarpa did restoration work, he preserved buildings and artworks in such a way as to encourage people to take care of the buildings and artworks, to provide a care that the buildings and artworks lacked sorely if they were neglected. He overturned the traditional approach to museum design (which often did nothing to hide its positivist origins, in the status of finds ascribed to the works) and proposed installations that become a sort of overall artwork, including as well as architecture, painting, sculpture, and so on.   In place of a neutral room, which presents the artworks in the illusion that nothing has been done to interfere with their figurative qualities, as if in an operating chamber, Scarpa designed specific rooms for exhibitions, aware that neutrality is impossible to attain, and devoted to the idea of using the architecture to amplify the "version of the world" communicated by the artworks. As far as the "compositional system" is concerned, Scarpa attempted to merge the architecture of late-baroque classicism, developed in the schools of fine arts, with the Japanism that constituted the complete antithesis of that school, its figurative counterpart. This influence of Oriental art upon architecture has often been underappreciated in the context of the modern movement, which counted on restoring a universal, objective, and scientific architecture — distant from the figurative arts, and closer to that form allied with engineering, which is pursued by functionalism. The continual interference between these two aspects — the "typological content" that focused on museum design, and the "compositional system" that was interwoven with the figurative arts — is a distinctive feature of Scarpa's architecture. The compositional system that combines the baroque with Japanism emerges from the explorations undertaken of those very same figurative arts, which constitute the "topic" of the exhibition/artworks created by Scarpa, in short, their typological content. It is precisely this proximity that makes the architectural language of Carlo Scarpa so remarkably effective from the referential point of view that it comes to constitute a body of full-fledged critical texts in figurative form.

4 — The architecture of Carlo Scarpa

It is interesting at this point to reconstruct the development of Scarpa's compositional system. If we base our study upon the current forms of historiography — which hold that modern archi-

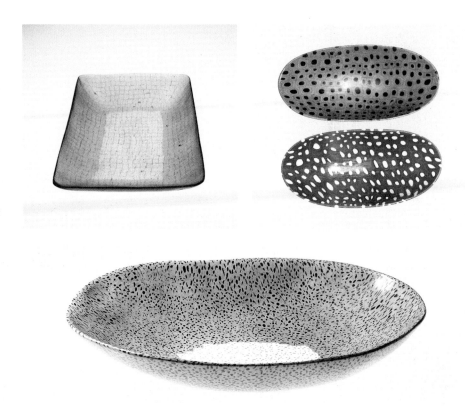

tecture can be traced back to the architecture of the Enlightenment, linking Ledoux with Le Corbusier, or else linking it to English domestic architecture, with specific reference to the Arts and Crafts Movement — it is not easy to find a place for the architecture of Carlo Scarpa. In the context of these approaches to architectural history and thought, one does not quite know where to place his projects and designs. Even an excessively specific historiography would prevent one from understanding their development, reducing his overall experience to an individual case (as is so often done). Scarpa's architectural experience can be broken up into three periods, sharply distinct in terms of research. The first period involved his development in the circle of artists and intellectuals that he met in Venice, at the Biennale, and at the Accademia di Belle Arti, or school of fine arts. These were circles that included also such philosophers of art as Sergio Bettini, Carlo Ludovico Ragghianti, and Giuseppe Mazzariol, who sustained that form of critical thought that had developed in Vienna, a form which included the principal, lesser, and applied arts in figured thought. The crafts experience that he had acquired in the workshops of Venini in Murano also forms part of this culture. It was in this environment, dominated by the figurative culture, that the links formed between

10, 11, 12.
Carlo Scarpa,
Glassware designed for
Venini, Venice, 1940;
once again we find
references to Japanese
art. The pictures are
reproduced from the
book by Marina
Barovier, *Murano.
Fantasie di vetro*,
Arsenale Editrice,
Venice, 1994.

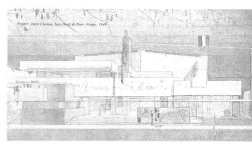

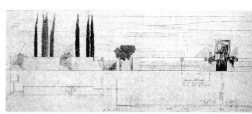

13.
Josef Hoffmann, *Stoclet Building*, Brussels, 1905-1911; there are many themes here that seem to foreshadow the work of Scarpa.

14.
Carlo Scarpa, *Cinema Astra*, San Donà di Piave (Venice), 1949; Scarpa's design is reminiscent of the figurative work of Klee.

15.
Rudolph Michael Schindler, *Pueblo Ribera Court*, La Jolla, 1923; in this work Schindler's work seems to foreshadow much of Scarpa's architecture.

16.
Carlo Scarpa, *Brion Family Monumental Tomb*; design of the wall that encloses the tomb.

17.
Carlo Scarpa, *Zoppas House*, Conegliano (Treviso), 1953.

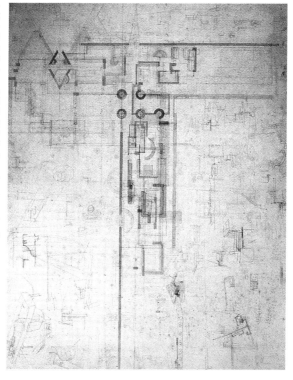

18.
Adolf Loos, *Kartner Bar*, Vienna, 1908.

the late-baroque of the Accademia di Belle Arti (among them, a certain professor Guido Cirilli, who was to bring Scarpa to the IUAV, Istituto Universitario di Architettura di Venezia, or University Department of Architecture, was a follower of Pietro da Cortona) and the Japanism of the plastic and figurative arts. Scarpa's interest in the Vienna Secession, and in the work of Josef Hoffmann, founder of the Wiener Werkstätte, was inspired by precisely this culture which, though with a different value, marked Otto Wagner's transition from his early work to the projects of his maturity. Scarpa's interest in Eastern culture, often overlooked by critics, was also what prompted him to pursue Frank Lloyd Wright's new spatial approach, found in the works of the second period, a spatial approach that vanished precisely when Scarpa, after touring the buildings designed and built by Wright, realized how different they were from his own architectural work. Marking the conclusion of this intellectual experience, we find that sort of "built treatise" of Scarpa's architecture that is the Brion Tomb. The compositional system of this second period, then, is marked by the transfer into architecture of a language that finds its most significant forms of expression first and foremost in the field of figurative arts. From my point of view, to say that this second period continues in the context of Wright's architecture means my sustaining that Scarpa found in that architecture a way of translating into architectural terms his culture as a figurative artist, that combination of classicism and Japanism that, prior to Wright, seemed better suited to the plastic arts than to architecture.

The third period was marked by Scarpa's continuing work to reduce his manner, and a growing awareness of his own contribution to a contemporary compositional system. Scarpa also found himself rendering more spare and organic a number of his previous projects, in the design work of this period. [5] He claimed that design develops through successive stages of clarification, progressively reducing the degree of complexity of the original configurations, which were dictated by the typological content of the project. He often recommended against fearing the formal complication of first designs, indeed to give it free rein, so as to be able to continue with the process of simplification. While many of the projects of the second period left this process of reduction incomplete, the projects of the third period — cut off by the tragic crash of Sendai in November of 1978 — are exemplary from this point of view. Scarpa imagined a "poor" architecture during these years, as if his compositional system had more in common with Adolf Loos, now, than with Josef Hoffmann or Frank Lloyd Wright.

5 — The histories of architecture

The ideological passion of the modern movement reconstructed its own histories, in the inevitable context of a specific political project. It is exceedingly difficult to place the work of Carlo Scarpa anywhere in that project. After the restrictions of that passion became looser, it became possible to single out approaches that, though they may have been exceedingly commonly practiced, did not correspond to "modern design." I believe that the current issues of architecture emerge from the declared relativity of the classical system. The idea of an "arbitrary beauty" — even though it may have been limited to the context of a rhetoric that opposed it to the greatly preferred "positive beauty," first theorized by Claude Perrault, and later by Christopher Wren — opened that debate between different compositional systems that has remained the overriding issue of the present. The system that Perrault proposed, with provocative intent, as an alternative to classicism, was Gothic, but later Johann Bernard Fischer von Erlach was to publish a treatise that set — alongside classical architecture — Arabic, Turkish, Chinese, Persian, Japanese, and other types of architecture. The idea that architecture must deal with the existence of a plurality of cultures, just as with the plurality of languages, was eluded by the "moderns" in two different ways: on the one hand,

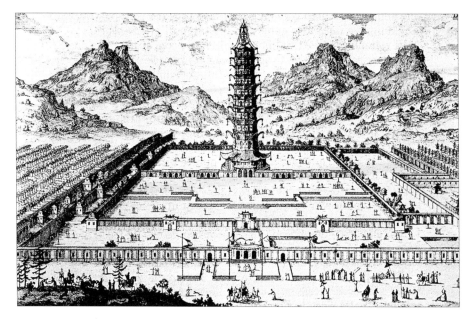

19.
Johann B. Fischer von
Erlach, *The Porcelain
Pagoda at Nanking*,
Vienna, 1721; Fischer
von Erlach's treatise
was the first to treat
buildings that
belonged to various
architectural cultures.

because, rather than accepting the relativity that was attributed to classicism, many chose to search for a different theory, a scientific theory, which could make architecture — truly — absolute and universal; and on the other hand because historicism interpreted the various "compositional systems" as different moments in the same historical evolution. The time aspect of this multiplicity of "compositional systems" was thus accentuated; thenceforth, they would be considered styles, in a way that at times would make them appear as fashions of the time, at times as features of the individual.

In some cases, in the most precarious of manners, a connection would appear between the compositional systems and the places and times that expressed them. When this happened, the extrahistorical vernacular, or the extrarchitectural "national style" would risk their very existence.

The relevance of Scarpa seems, in my estimation, to be due to the figurative complexity of his compositional system. He bears witness to a paradoxical condition that is typical of architectural culture. While it is precisely the reflections of those who treat the grammar of architecture that sets the stage for this confrontation among the various compositional systems, the prohibition implemented by the modern movement against that grammar deprived the architectural culture of the tools it needed to deal with the complexity engendered by that confrontation. A culture that considered architecture as a craft, a technique, could never have promoted this comparative approach, even though the erroneous interpre-

18

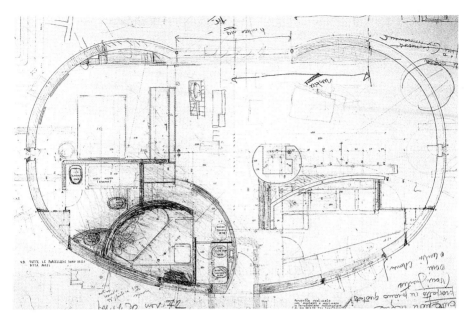

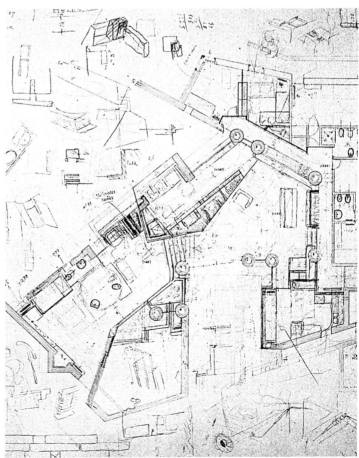

20.
Carlo Scarpa, *De Benedetti House*, Rome, 1965-1972; when Scarpa was designing this building often commented on the project in terms of the architecture of Francesco Borromini.

21.
Carlo Scarpa, *Ottolenghi House*, Mure di Bardolino (Verona), 1975-1979.

tation of this pluralism as if it were an "event," holds it to be an indicator of the definitive decline of that architecture. Dealing with the pluralism of architectural cultures, therefore, is an "action" carried out by a subject, and is therefore the expression of a level of development attained by the architecture of classicism which, once it had become an institution, made this possible. This process sinks its roots deep in the architectural thought that first examined this historicist pluralism, in the complexity of a culture that intertwines mature classicism, mannerism, and the baroque. There is, in the current of European influence of the work of Borromini (to use the Italian, in "borrominismo"), the intention of developing a problematic relationship with non-classical historical compositional systems. If we agree that these figurative contaminations are the source of the design of Scarpa's fragments, then we can grasp the degree to which his architecture faces up — in a non-stylistic manner — to the issue of the pluralism of compositional systems. Carlo Scarpa's resistance to the bans and restrictions of modern design, his radical non-conformity, and likewise his marginal status — all these factors allowed him to be well ahead of the curve in dealing with the problems we now face and in indicating some possible solutions. Who could deny that those of his compositions that work through dissociation are in some sense forerunners of the disjoint creations of the deconstructivists? That his precious details/fragments are in some way forerunners of certain compositional work of Japanese architecture? That his interest in the autonomy of the façade points to a special attention to civic architecture?

Perhaps Scarpa failed to identify as themes these examples of architectural byplay, these quotations that dropped freely from his vast range of figurative culture, and perhaps only a profound familiarity with the classical system made the complexity of his compositions in any way governable. If one accepts — as I believe he did — the "conventional," but not subjective, nature of the "architectural system," rather than "submitting to its pluralism ," then one can begin to grasp its compatibility and consistency with that "universal grammar" about which architectural treatises theorize, drawn from a great array of different bodies of architecture.

Indeed, languages are based upon "conventions," and certainly their pluralism does nothing to persuade us that they are subjective, because it fails, simply, to establish that they are objective. The fact that languages can be translated one into another, through an understanding of their grammatical structure, allows us to study them comparatively. An oral culture, or a dialect that lacks the institutional structure that is given by the production of literature and of a written grammar, would not be able to undertake such comparative study. Architectural culture in its current state need not submit to the pluralism of compositional systems, nor need it reject that pluralism. The correct way of posing the question lies, in my opinion, in interpreting this comparison in terms of that "universal grammar" of the "architectural system" that classicism has pursued now for so many centuries. This does not mean, of course, that we should camouflage contemporary architecture with images taken from a misunderstanding of classicism; rather it means "adapting" the "universal grammar" of the classical system in a manner consistent with the local architectural cultures. I believe that it is possible to interpret the last period of Scarpa's architecture in this light: it is an architecture committed to recovering the new spatial approach that Frank Lloyd Wright had taken from the Japanese culture in the context of that "universal grammar." When speaking about the design for the Banca Popolare of Verona, Scarpa expressed quite clearly how grateful he would be if architectural critics were able to recognize the references and connections to classical architecture.[6]

Notes

[1] Making "room," which English treats differently from "space," used more commonly in other languages, is distinguished by Heidegger from the abstract space of modern technology. It is no accident that in English "room" also means the basic unit of a building, and that in this book I indicate the room as the fundamental proposition of architectural "language." Cfr. M. Heidegger, *Die Kunst und der Raum*, St. Gallen, Erker Verlag, 1969.

[2] M. Heidegger, *Holzwege*, Frankfurt a. M., Klostermann, 1950.

[3] W. Benjamin, *Der Begriff der Kunstkritik in der deutschen Romantik*, in *Gesammelte Schriften*, I, 1, Frankfurt a. M., Suhrkamp Verlag, 1974.

[4] I have written extensively about this matter in the study I have devoted to Carlo Scarpa, in an attempt to explain his design method to students; please refer to the chapter, "La coscienza architettonica," in S. Los, *Carlo Scarpa architetto e poeta*, Venice, Cluva, 1967.

[5] Concerning this final period of Scarpa's architecture, one can consult: F. Dal Co, "La maturità di Carlo Scarpa," in *Piranesi*, n. 3, vol. 2, Ljubljana, 1993.

[6] This was not the only instance in which Scarpa wished to refer to classical architecture. In fact, he said: "I want to confess: I would be very pleased if a critic were to discover, in my work, certain intentions that I have always had. This is to say, a powerful determination to remain within tradition, but window using capitals and columns, because those are just no longer possible to use." C. Scarpa, "Mille cipressi," lecture delivered in Madrid in summer 1978, in F. Dal Co, G. Mazzariol (ed.), *Carlo Scarpa. Complete Works*, Milan-London, 1984.

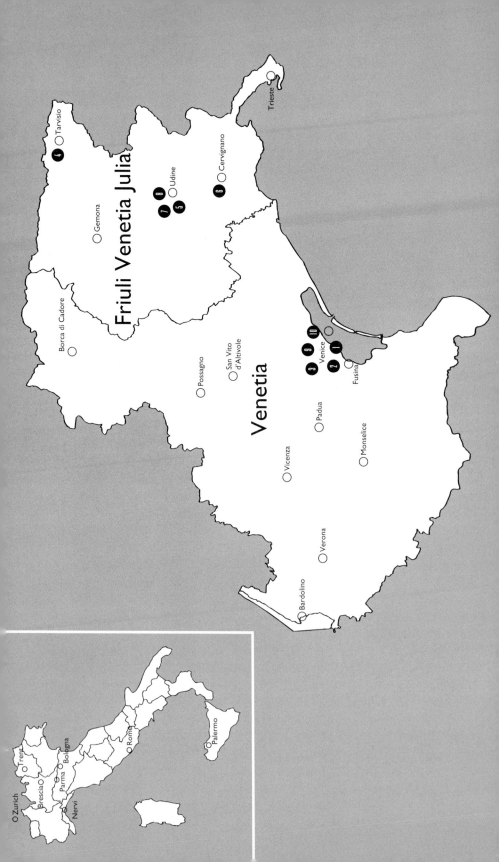

The heritage of Wright and artistic culture

In this early period, Scarpa's attention was focused primarily on new work that was involved with the area of the figurative arts. The restoration of Ca' Foscari, the work he did for Venini, his working relationships with museums and with the Biennale, and even his friendships with Arturo Martini and Mario De Luigi, and his closeness with such critics as Carlo Ludovico Ragghianti, Giuseppe Mazzariol, Sergio Bettini, Licisco Magagnato, and others, all indicate his great involvement in the artistic culture of those years. Scarpa experienced directly the innovative state of tensions of a form of knowledge which included the increasing exploration of Eastern figurative culture; it was precisely while searching for an architectural translation of this that he discovered the work of Frank Lloyd Wright. That Japanism that reached Europe through the expositions of the nineteenth century were particularly important to the Vienna Secession movement, Art Nouveau, and the renewal of figurative languages in general. It would be difficult to understand fully Scarpa's interest in Wright's work without recognizing the need to which his work offered a fulfilling figurative solution. Wright represented an architectural response to a desire for new concepts of space that was widespread in the context of the figurative arts.

Many of these early projects were developed in collaboration with Angelo Masieri, who learned to appreciate the great American architect through Scarpa. These were the years in which Bruno Zevi was familiarizing the Italians with organic architecture, but the experimentation of Scarpa was particularly unique. Sustained by his deep-rooted figurative culture, it differs sharply from the experimentation of the many architects who imitated Wright.

|

Renovation of Ca' Foscari
1935-37
Renovation of the "Aula Magna" or Great Hall
(with *V. Pastor*)
1954-56
Venice, Dorsoduro 3246

In his restoration of Ca' Foscari, the building that houses the University, Scarpa indicated an exceedingly original approach to restoring buildings. His project was to give the building once again, after the alterations made during the eighteenth and nineteenth centuries, an image that in some sense was appropriate to the original. In a period of false reconstructions and camouflaging, the critical approach of Scarpa's project aroused considerable debate. Aside from designing the furnishings of the chancellor's

office and the other offices, Scarpa suggested an approach to the renovation of the windows that was later widely used in the restoration of very old palazzi: he recessed the glass with respect to the Gothic arcade, making the design of the window frames independent of the original outer structure. Overlooking the Grand Canal, moreover, he designed a glazed inner door that reflected the moving water, producing an ever-changing light in constant motion. On the main floor, a system of movable panels could be used to isolate the hall for conferences and lectures, while on the   was the "Aula Magna"

with a gallery for students. Scarpa was commissioned to transform the "Aula Magna" into a lecture hall. His design called for a screen in wood and glass — consisting of a series of that supported a ceiling made of a grating structure, and a series of movable shutters, or partitions — which would separate the space of the hall from an interior hallway. The design of these wooden elements represents a refined version of the supports designed by Wright for his studio in Taliesin East in Wisconsin. The uprights were built with different hardwoods, salvaged from the preceding demolition.

2

Capovilla Family Tomb
1943-44
Venice, cemetery of San Michele in Isola, precinct XX

This project dealt with a monumental subject, of the sort that particularly interested Scarpa. It was a project in which his artistic education caused him to waver between the formal abstraction that characterizes the funerary culture of the Enlightenment and the figurative depiction that is typical of the Italian sepulchral tradition. The slab of botticino marble, slightly hollowed out, terminates at the top with stylized wings. In the middle of the stele is inset a bas-relief of the "Deposition," which belonged to the client family.

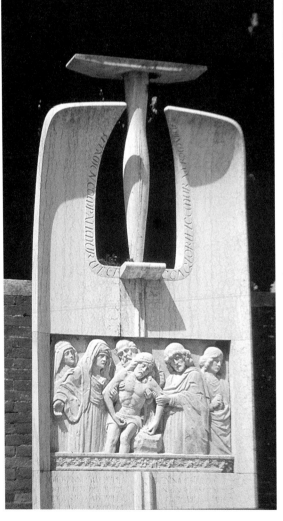

3

Renovation of the Galleries of the Accademia
(with *V. Pastor*)
1945 onward
Venice, Dorsoduro 1050, Campo della Carità
Telephone 39.41.5222247

Vittorio Moschini, superintendent of the Galleries of the Accademia, convinced Scarpa to work on a ongoing joint project that began in 1945 and was not to be completed until 1959. The renovation required the adoption of new criteria of exhibition, so that the works were displayed by style, era, and theme. In order to give an unobstructed view of the works, Scarpa suggested placing the radiators in the middle of each room; he designed skylights in the church of the Carità, which stood adjacent to the Galleries, and which housed fifteenth-century paintings and a triptych by Vivarini and D'Alemagna, benches, and a display case for sculptures by Canova; later on, he reopened a number of windows that had been sealed up in the nineteenth century, replacing the coffer ceiling and the cloth wallpaper with plaster. The renovation of the entrance-hall, with the glazed inner entrance door, the counter, and the display panels, dates from 1952.

4

Banca Cattolica del Veneto
(with *A. Masieri*)
1947-48
Tarvisio (Udine), Via Roma 2
Telephone 39.428.40206

Angelo Masieri had been one of Scarpa's students; when he was commissioned, with his father, to design a bank in Tarvisio, near Udine, he called on his "professor" to help in a working partnership that was to go on to other projects as well. The plan for this two-story building reveals — both in the use of materials and in the composition of volumes — a great interest in the architecture of Frank Lloyd Wright. It differs from more traditional types of mountain architecture in that it adopted a nearly flat ceiling — a cold roof — that would accumulate snow, so as to prevent the formation of ice in the gutter system, improving the building's insulation. On the ground floor are the offices, with a large hall for the public, while on the main floor was the residence of the bank president. The building subsequently underwent renovations that partially changed the interior layout.

5

Giacomuzzi House
(with *A. Masieri*)
1947-50
Udine, Via Marinoni 11/13, c/o
COPECO
Telephone 39.432.503708

This building presents a broad and thoroughly articulated distribution of rooms on the ground floor, and a main floor, opening out onto large terraces, which one can reach from the front hall via a staircase. The limited lot, surrounding by buildings that hem it in, conditioned the design of the building's plan which reflects, in the continuous series of rooms, the new sense of space taken from Wright's work. The continuity between exterior and interior hearkens back to the potential offered by Japanese gardens, making the available spaces seem larger. Particularly noteworthy is the wooden staircase, immediately visible upon entering the home.

6

Bortolotto House
(with *A. Masieri*)
1950-52
Cervignano (Udine), Via Udine 52
Telephone 39.432.32169. Private residence, which can
be viewed from outside.

For the design of this house, Scarpa and Masieri
had separately developed two designs; they later developed the design by Masieri, which the
client had preferred. The house, which is located
in Cervignano, between Palmanova and Grado,
is built close to an enormous tree, and blends
the culture of Venetian country houses with an
acute awareness of the work done by Wright in
the context of organic architecture. This building, gathered entirely beneath a single broad roof
which is visible from the road, consitutes a tes-
timonial to the sensibilities of Scarpa and Masieri
for the location. The building, in fact., was designed with a view to the local climate; the long
wall protects the garden and the courtyard
from the winter winds.

7

Romanelli House (now Marzullo House)
(with *A. Masieri*)
1950-55
Udine, Via F. Filzi 2,
Telephone 39.432.532570. Private residence,
which can be viewed from outside.

Scarpa completed this house — which he designed together with Masieri — with the architect Angelo Morassuti. The modelling of the roof, the corner windows, the spatial continuity, the asymmetrical composition of the floor plan, the baroque counterpoint produced by the intersection of two horizontal figures in the design of the floor plan, and the linking of the exterior and the interior, constitute the principal features of this project, which reflects Scarpa's interest in Wright's translation of figurative Japanism, which spread through Western culture from the second half of the nineteenth century onward.

8
Veritti Tomb
(with *A. Masieri*)
1951
Udine, Cemetery of San Vito, Via Martini 2
Telephone 39.432.530502

This is a grassy and flowered enclosure, which can be reached through a circular entrance: a room with an open ceiling is intended as a place for quiet meditation. Once again, the influence of Oriental architecture — Chinese and Japanese — is filtered from the teachings of Frank Lloyd Wright. Part of the enclosure is covered by the roof made of a large disc of oxidized bronze, set on two metal supports located in the wall and also suspended from a fastening supported on a metal beam. These details at the points of attachment and the dissociation of the elements and partis are indications of the compositional system of Scarpa's architecture.

9

Entrance and garden-patio of the Biennale
1952
Venice, Castello Gardens, Biennale

The entrance consists of a fence and a removable cabin, set on a concrete foundation. The wells were made of iron and wooden frameworks that supported the wired double-glass windows. The canvas roof, leaf-shaped, was supported by a lenticular structure made of iron and wood. All that survives now are the permanent sections made of concrete.

In the central pavilion, the elimination of one room freed up an open space, which Scarpa redesigned by placing a curved cantilevered roof upon three cement pillars. In the walls, he uncovered the brick structure and the flooring, made up of washed concrete slabs, revolves around a number of small basins of water. The presence of Japanese culture can be detected in the treatment of the garden-patio, in the materials, and in the use of water.

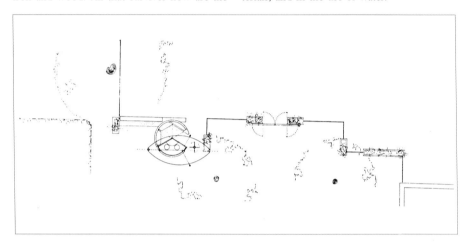

10

Historical sections of the Correr Museum
1953
Venice, Saint Mark's Square 52
Telephone 39.41.5225625. Closed Tuesdays.

The selection of the rooms, which were to become so many chapters in the architectural text, and in those rooms, the selection of the places and supports used to display this exhibition of mementoes of the history of the Republic of Venice, offers a perfect demonstration of the art of "showing" that so marks Scarpa's architecture. This is an architecture conceived as a instrument of communication, making eloquent every object exhibited. Coins, weapons, costumes, banners, portraits, et al., summon up the image of a Venice that expresses an evocative visual cultural identity. Scarpa's discourse proceeds from one room to the next in an exemplary manner, recounting the ups and downs of a long-past history, in the "words" of architecture.

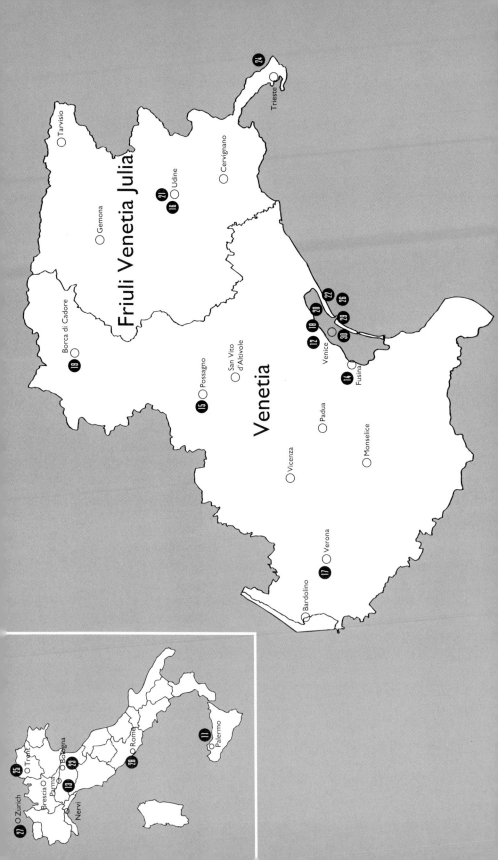

Friuli Venetia Julia

Tarvisio

Udine
Cervignano
Gemona
Trieste

Borca di Cadore

San Vito
d'Altivole
Possagno

Venetia

Venice
Fusina

Padua

Vicenza

Monselice

Verona

Bardolino

Roma
Palermo

Zurich
Trent
Bologna
Brescia
Parma
Nervi

Toward a critical architecture

Carlo Scarpa, in his second period, focused on the design of museum spaces, installations of exhibitions, and composite architecture, in which the building blended with the works that it contained. From this point onward, the critical capacity of the architecture became recognizable, along with its tendency to endow a museum with as much eloquence as its works of art possess. If there had been no continuity with the figurative arts, if the architecture had been radically different from the painting and the sculpture involved, this work by Scarpa could never have existed. If, on the other hand, there is a figurative thought and knowledge, then those forms of knowledge would find, in the synergy of the installations, the intensity of Scarpa. These works hearken back to that great moment of figurative art that the painter/architects and the sculptor/architects of the early Renaissance inaugurated with the invention of design by drawing. Everyone knows just how important such design was for Scarpa, and just how much he contributed to the innovation of its use in architectural projects: a design conceived as a system of notation, much as a musical score, to be used freely and in common by painters, sculptors, and architects. Those who tour the great masterpieces of this period should ponder the originality of this conception, which underlies the work of Scarpa. It is as if Scarpa, having discovered a new and unexplored system for linking fields of knowledge that had long been separated, was capable of activating potential forms of communication that architecture had too long ignored. One might say that Scarpa made use of his ability as an installation maker in homes and offices as well; walls, stairways, roofs, and windows all appear, making the context eloquent, displaying its figure as if it were a work of art.

II

Museum installation of Palazzo Abatellis for the Regional Gallery of Sicily
(with R. Calandra)
1953-54
Palermo, Via Alloro 4

Palazzo Abatellis was built between 1490 and 1526 by Matteo Carnelivari; after it had sustained a fair amount of damage over the centuries, in 1943 a bomb destroyed the arcade, the portico, the southwest wing, and the western tower. The commission was assigned to Scarpa in the wake of a major exhibition on Antonello da Messina, which he supervised in Messina; Professor Calandra toured the Correr Museum and realized what important architectural work on museum installations Scarpa had been doing.

When this project was completed, the architect received a Premio Nazionale, or National Award, for a project that Walter Gropius described as "the finest installation of a museum that I have seen in all my life." The building, with a rectangular floor plan, is entirely directed toward an interior courtyard, upon which an arcade faces. Scarpa preserved the paving of the courtyard, which employed river cobbles; the pavement is divided by diagonal lines that call attention to the corners, salient points of the interior. In the façade, Scarpa placed window frames behind the arcade, on a different plane from that described by their arabesque motifs, lest the frames interfere with the arabesques. This simple necessity to respect the old structure and to preserve its design led Scarpa to the tech-

nique of separating the plane of the opening from the plane of the casements. And so he transferred to Palermo an exceedingly Venetian way of dealing with space, as a series of distinct and superimposed planes. The works to be placed on exhibit were selected carefully, so as to give the museum a sense of lightness, while the other works were placed in storage on special sliding racks, so that they remained easily accessible. What is most striking about this work is the method of installation, the way in which the paintings and sculpture were given three-dimensional frameworks. Along with his instinctive sensibility for the works, which allowed him to select the most appropriate lighting, materials, and colors, Scarpa displayed a remarkable and extensive artistic culture; the canvases, for example, are placed on supports so that there is a space between the support and the wall, allowing a slight column of air to circulate behind it, while the frames are placed so as to permit them to be inspected easily. Scarpa imposes a sort of obligatory itinerary, inviting the visitor to stop and ponder the features that Scarpa considered most important. This effort is successful, arousing interest in even the most apathetic visitors, awakening curiosity, forcing them to walk all the way around a sculpture or convincing them to shift a painting on its frame in order to see it with the best lighting. A new open interior stairway, with stone steps with hexagonal cross-sections supported by a steel beam, leads from the ground floor to the ancient monumental staircase that leads up to the

main floor. Palazzo Abatellis represents an example of architectural poetry at the same time that if functions as a piece of exceedingly acute and perceptive architectural analysis. The architecture takes on an hermeneutic function, as its ability to interpret helps to exhibit the figurative works that were displayed within it, suggesting a brand-new approach to criticism.

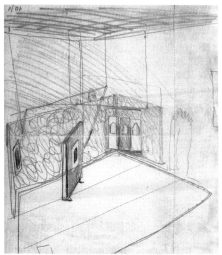

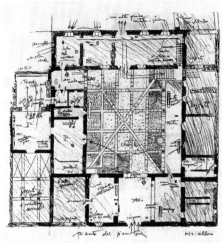
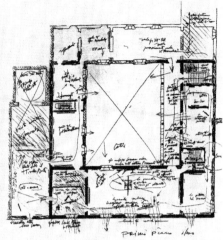

12

Pavilion of Venezuela

(with *V. Pastor, G. D'Agaro, Marchesin, C. Maschietto*)

1954-56

Venice, Castello Gardens, Biennale

This work can be viewed only from outside; it has been heavily remodeled.

This little pavilion takes its inspiration, in the interplay between the two slightly offset halls along the gallery, from the paintings of Klee. Quite often, Scarpa's composition is based upon pairs of correlated elements; his figurative approach demonstrates the skill he has acquired in "handling the design by drawing." The portico that overlooks the park and which concludes the gallery features a number of panels that can seal it off entirely, by rotating upon pivots, which is a sophisticated piece of work to find in a form of architecture decidedly quite distant from "machine esthetics." The modifiable space, produced by the mechanisms of the movable walls, is reminiscent — even more than in the work of Wright — of the transformability of space in Japanese architecture. Likewise, the rich and eloquent complexity of the detailing hearkens back to the structural techniques of Japanese carpentry. A separate discussion should be devoted to the natural lighting, filtered through the green curtain created by the branches of the large trees, a light that penetrates through the long corner openings in the roof. The walls, illuminated by midday light, are entirely usable for exhibition.

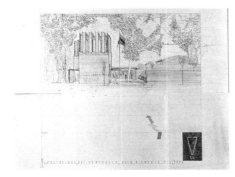
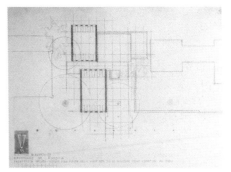

13

Council Hall of the Administrative Provincial Government
(with *V. Pastor, G. D'Agaro*)
1955-56
Parma, Piazzale della Pace 1

The design of this hall is noteworthy in particular because of the cunning coordination of: the furnishings; the lighting, both natural and artificial; and the organization of space. Scarpa's compositional system followed, during this period, the paradigms of a De Stijl "order," which governs the syntactical sequence of the various figurative elements. The frescoes on the walls were done by the Venetian painter Armando Pizzinato.

14
Layout of a Campground at Fusina
1957
Venice, Fusina
Telephone 39.41.5470055

The plan for this campground consitutes a unique episode in the overall context of Scarpa's work. It consists of a continuous wall, in bare bricks, that establishes on either side, through a particular shape, the complex of spaces that makes up the various facilities of the campground. The zigzagging course of the wall is reminiscent — as are other of Scarpa's projects — of certain figurative efforts by Klee.

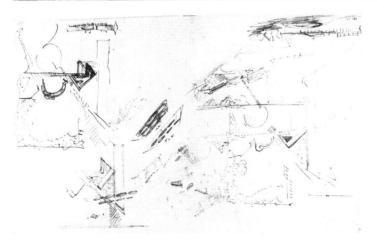

15

Expansion of the Canova Sculpture Gallery
(with V. *Pastor*)
1955-57
Possagno (near Treviso), Piazza Canova
Telephone 39.423.544323

The Commission of Fine Arts, in 1955, commissioned Scarpa to expand the Sculpture Gallery (Gipsoteca) of Possagno, in celebration of the second centennial of the birth of Antonio Canova, a native of the town. The expansion of the existing Sculpture Gallery, a building with a basilican floor plan erected between 1831 and 1836 by Giuseppe Segusini, was dictated by the need to display adequately the original plaster models, the casts, a number of marble works, and a number of rough versions in terracotta — at the time this material was rudely piled up. Scarpa built a "cascade" roof that, starting from a high room, ran between two converging walls, descending with a glass wall toward a basin of water, from which the sunlight reflected a bright light toward Canova's masterpiece, "The Three Graces." The roof follows the downward slope of the floors, which multiply the points of view as they descend, arranging the sculptures in settings such that the constrast is heightened between the abstract whiteness of the plasters and the animated realism of the female

46

body, reclining or erect. The modelling of an articulated and variable luminous space provides the rationale for the openings in the structural shell, which Scarpa designed by snipping off the corners of the rooms so as to create transparent trihedrons.

These openings reduce the dazzling effect that comes from the contrast — present in the normal windows at the center of the wall — between the light from the opening and the shadows of the wall that surrounds that opening. In the situation as Scarpa has designed it, the light source always encounters a perpendicular diffusor plane, which creates the best possible conditions for lighting the space. The angling

47

and shape of these windows produces a remarkable architectural effect: "I wanted to cut out the blue of the sky," Carlo Scarpa was later to say about them.

Of the two walls that shape the new Sculpture Gallery, the massive outer wall reflects light upon the display area and, providing the sculptures with an appropriate background, determines its figure outline. The other wall is transparent, and formed by a framework of steel pillars and architraves, partly glassed in and partly

formed of courses of "pietra tenera" from Vicenza. Each statue has a very precise place, with respect to the overall space and to the light that pours in — at times with glaring violence, at other times softly and faintly — modelling the plasters on display, modifying them over the course of the day, with the changing seasons, and the variations in weather. For this reason, Giuseppe Mazzariol spoke of "personalities in stone": the spectator has the impression of living with these creatures.

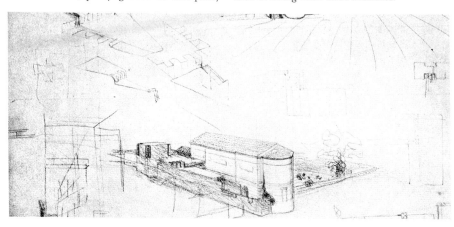

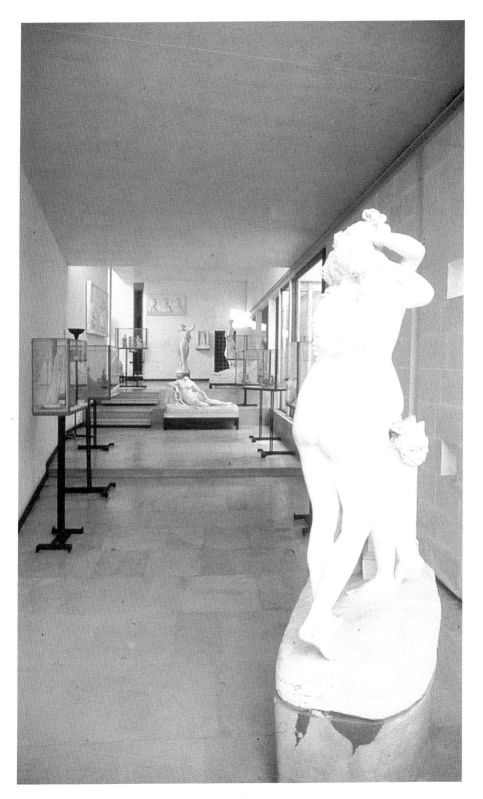

16

Veritti House

(with F. Marconi, C. Maschietto)

1955-61

Udine, Viale Duodo

Telephone 39.432.26638. Private residence, which can be viewed from outside.

Carlo Scarpa received this commission from a lawyer named Luigi Veritti, a relative of Angelo Masieri, with whom Scarpa had done so much research into the architecture of Frank Lloyd Wright. The context of this project presented two orders of difficulty: the elongated shape of the lot, and the indeterminate nature of the area, no longer nature, but not yet urban. When faced with particularly narrow spaces, Scarpa generally suggested building with curved construction. "At one point," he once wrote, "there may be very narrow passages, as long as the space widens further on, and this can be obtained by curving the walls." To avoid having to refer with straight-line structures to the axis imposed by the shape of the lot, Scarpa made use first of a plan consisting of two circles, then the current, more compact solution. The house consists of a single volume, sheltered by a semi-cylindrical wall that encloses it toward the north, like a shell, excluding the north wind and the occasional unwanted gaze, and entirely open toward the south, so as to capture the sunlight and so as to offer a view of a less built-up area. The circular shape, broken up by the polyhedric progression of the glass wall, is completed by the outline of the basin of water,

which reflects the jutting façade, while the winter garden emerges like a crystal from the wall. The space is punctuated by triangular cement pillars, formed of stacked, L-shaped, modular elements with rounded-off corners, covered on the interior by decorated slabs with prism-shaped motifs, which can be removed so as to gain access to the ducts for the various heating systems. Along with the block of cylinders for the staircase and the chimneys, the hollow pillars for the various pipe systems constitute a recurrent theme in the work of Carlo Scarpa, a theme that has since been developed in a systematic manner by Louis I. Kahn.

The specific configuration of these pillars avoids the alignment that is imposed by the grid of load-bearing structures. Scarpa wished to avoid the skeletal structure, that regular web of pilasters that would have pigeonholed his work into the context of rational architecture.

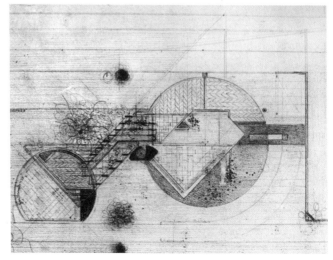

17

Restoration and Installation of the Museum of Castelvecchio

(with C. Maschietto, A. Rudi)

1956-64

Verona, Castelvecchio

Telephone 39.45.592985. Closed Mondays.

On the occasion of the exhibition "From Altichiero to Pisanello," held in 1957, Licisco Magagnato, director of the Civic Museum of Verona, commissioned Scarpa to restore only the "Reggia." With selective digs and creative demolitions, Scarpa attempted to isolate and uncover the various historical strata of the complex. He attempted to untangle the intricate remains of the various eras of construction so as to make the building itself one giant artifact or find, whose various phases of expansion and structural modifications were revealed by the various phases of restoration. More than a theory of restoration, he was interested in "historical clarity," so that history might become recognizable through the orderly coexistence of the various fragments. Scarpa thus found himself working on a building that had been restored in 1923 by the architect Arnaldo Forlati who, in order to transform the castle into a museum, had dressed it with an antique "mask," replacing the façade of the barracks with a collage of Gothic artifacts uncovered in the wake of a flood — thus transforming a military building into a pseudo-medieval palazzo with an Italian-style garden. "At Castelvecchio everything was fake," Scarpa later said in 1978 at Madrid, in a lecture, concerning the façade of the courtyard. "I decided to adopt a number of overriding values, in order to upset the unnatural symmetry: Gothic called for that symmetry broken up, as

Gothic and especially Venetian Gothic is anything but symmetrical." He tried out a number of different ideas. In the end he left the façade apparently intact, even though its "unnatural symmetry" had been "disturbed" by a number of changes. First of all he moved the entrance, shifting it away from the center of the façade. He wished for the façade to appear clearly as a tacked-on piece of stage setting and therefore, as he had done in other projects, he separated it from the grid of the window casements,

which provided a link to the interior. The façade remains in a close-knit dialogue with the exterior, with the courtyard, via a number of jutting elements: pavement, votive chapel, and entrance wall. Here more than anywhere else, one can see the degree to which Scarpa's architecture is made up of juxtapositions. These are different materials, different stories that, when brought close together though kept rigorously separate, begin a sort of dialogue. That is the reason for the fractures: the pavements, as if they were carpets, are kept separate from the edge of the walls, the walls are separated from the ceilings, and the ceilings are subdivided. The various materials that mark the various rooms make this perception tactile as well as visual. In the last bay, which has been demolished in order to uncover the hidden stratifications, Scarpa identified the place in which the entire project came together in a sort of synthesis, where he placed the statue of Cangrande della Scala. In the point of the greatest historical complexity and interweaving — hoisted up on a very high slab supported by a cement corbel and set at a dynamic angle to the wall — the statue was intentionally made particularly visible from every point throughout the castle by artifical loopholes, thus injecting into the itinerary of the exhibition the constant and almost sinister tension of the "historic" gaze of the ironic Scaliger duke. Facing the great fountain,

which is located in a large basin full of water, there is another one, and Scarpa playfully inserts in the center of it a little drinking fountain, so as to turn the minor everyday act of taking a drink into a small ceremony. Only one person at a time can reach the drinking fountain to place one foot on its single small support. Near the entrance, nearly hidden by an oblique cement wall, a small casket or monumental chapel extends out of the façade, in which precious Longobard artifacts are displayed, lit from above by a small opening at the top. The exterior of the sacellum is sheathed with many little blocks of "prun" stone, in various hues and shades of color, ranging from white to red, with an alternation of rough and smooth surfaces. The interior is lined with bottle-green satin-finish natural plaster: the pavement is made of terracotta, with iron edges. The museum space is organized into an enfilade of rooms dating from

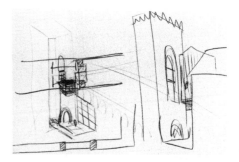

the Napoleonic era, which Scarpa relieved of their original rigidity, now indicated solely by the long steel beam that seems to stretch continuously the length of the building. The caisson ceiling was evoked by Scarpa in four reinforced-cement architraves, which the steel architrave supplies with a central point of support.

The four infills are colored. The rest is treated with intentionally unassuming materials, alternating with some rather elaborate episodes, as a framework and commentary to the works on display. An arched door with a sliding steel gate leads to the great open space where the statue of Cangrande stands. The gate, like many oth-

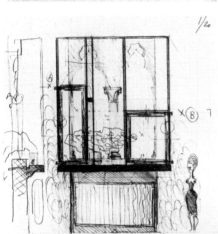

ers found in the building, is formed by the interweaving of thin plates of iron, joined so as to create an orthogonal grid — with warp and weft — that reproduces a pattern that Scarpa had previously used for the Olivetti store in Venice. A welter of steps at various levels, reminiscent of the work of Piranesi, in troweled concrete, edged with flat structural shapes in iron, leads to the western courtyard, beyond the shared wall. After touring, in the halls of the "Reggia," the paintings and statues from the period that ranges from the Middle Ages to the end of the fifteenth century, and after crossing through the tower of the "Mastio," or keep, one returns to the former barracks — on the main floor — passing by the statue of Cangrande, with the possibility of walking across the battlemented walls, as well; the tour ends in the gallery that displays paintings dating from the fifteenth to the eighteenth centuries. Lastly, we should make some mention of a number of systems employed in displaying the paintings. Scarpa designed all of the exhibition equipment and supports, generally made of iron and wood. Scarpa went beyond the simple task of lining the walls with paintings, and oversaw the framing, as well as attending to a number of technical details involved in exhibiting different types of works; he created spaces and determined juxtapositions, making use of perspective to trigger realizations in the visitor. In particular, he oversaw the orientation of the paintings with respect to the side lighting from the windows to the north as well as to the south.

18

Olivetti Showroom
(with G. *D'Agaro*, C. *Maschietto*)
1957-58
Venice, Saint Mark's Square
Telephone 39.41.5235955

Carlo Scarpa was commissioned to renovate the showroom in Saint Mark's Square after he was announced as the winner, in 1956, together with Ludovico Quaroni, of the Olivetti Prize for architecture. His nomination for the prize was hotly supported by the critic Bruno Zevi with a view to enhancing the architecture of Frank Lloyd Wright. The site poses a number of

thorny problems: a long and narrow space, poorly lit, but in an intriguing corner location. The space is fairly tall — about four meters — and does not lend itself to a second story; Scarpa therefore designed a remarkable marble staircase and two low balconies that do not interfere with the perception of the room as a whole. This perception is integral to the gradual modulation of the lighted space, with large windows opening onto the square through the portico. The space can always be seen and perceived in its entirety; the mezzanine floor is illuminated by mandorla-shaped openings, as if they were eyes looking out over the square. The entrance, at the side, almost seems to preannounce the asymmetry of the interior arrangement of space. The little entrance-hall is dominated by a gilded nude, by Alberto Viani, reflected in the water in a basin made of black Belgian marble, slightly raised from the floor. Further along, the stairway made of suspended slabs of marble amounts to a neoplastic deconstruction of Michelangelo's stairway in the Laurentian Library; Scarpa broke up the prismatic

space with an informal cascade of steps that seem to race downward. The stairway itself, made of "Aurisina" marble, leads to the mezzanine which, through the balcony, links and distinguishes the various spatial aspects on the interior of the store. The overall artificial lighting is done with vertical bands of glazed glass that contain fluorescent lamps, while local lighting is done with small ebony lamps that run on long stainless steel rods.

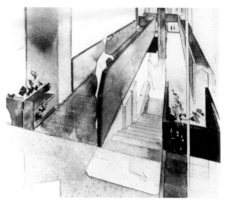

19

Church for a Holiday Village Owned by ENI

(with E. *Gellner*)
1959
Borca di Cadore (Belluno), SNAM
Holiday Center

Scarpa's work on this small church, which he de- signed with Gellner, can be detected in a number of details and in the steel spire, reminiscent of the bell tower that he designed for the parish church of Torre di Mosto in 1948, and of a number of similar pieces of formal research by Wright. The large wooden roof is supported by concrete struts with chains formed by steel cables, inclined in such a way as to be perpendicular.

20

Remodelling of the Gallery of Paintings of the Correr Museum

(with *V. Pastor, G. D'Agaro*)
1957-60
Venice, Saint Mark's Square 52
Telephone 39.41.5225625. Closed Tuesdays.

The remodeled version designed by Scarpa emphasized the alignment of the halls that overlook Saint Mark's Square, through the windows of the Procuratie Nuove. The little wooden easels that support the paintings are arranged along a line of perspective following the line of doors and windows. The sequence of figures formed by this succession of rooms is interrupted by other rooms that have been placed along this axis in order to give the visitor a wider range of choices. The proof of Scarpa's remarkable gift for grasping the underlying architectural concept lies in the fact that here he has designed a renovation that so perfectly fits into the context that a visitor can easily think of the halls — which existed previously — as having been expressly designed for this installation.

21
Zilio Family Tomb
1960
Udine, Cemetery of San Vito, Via Martini 2
Telephone 39.432.530502

This tomb is located in the cemetery of Udine and was commissioned by Miss Zilio, for whom Scarpa had already remodelled an apartment. The tomb consists of a wall formed by a composition of slabs of polished "botticino" marble and rough-hewn "pietra d'Istria," enclosed in an iron cornice; upon the wall is engraved and gilded the legend "Zilio." The face of the letters, which appears in other projects as well, was designed by Scarpa. At the center is a Franciscan cross, whose configuration was designed by Scarpa in many different variants; it is made of twinned cylinders in burnished muntz metal.

22

Querini-Stampalia Foundation. Remodelling of the ground floor and the garden

(with C. Maschietto)
1961-63
Venice, Castello 4778, Campo Santa
Maria Formosa
Telephone 39.41.5203433

Giuseppe Mazzariol, a friend of Carlo Scarpa's and his colleague at the Istituto Universitario di Architettura of Venice (where he taught Architectural History), was the director of the Querini-Stampalia Foundation during the early Sixties. When it was decided that restoration work should be done, Mazzariol assigned the project of remodelling the ground floor to Scarpa. The ground floor had been put entirely out of commission by periodic flooding; Scarpa was also commissioned to renovate the courtyard of a sixteenth-century palazzo, which contained the library and galleries. A renovation done in the nineteenth century had completely distorted the original spatial structure of the building, and it was now necessary to restore that spatial structure to

the building with a kind of critical project. As in many other cases, Scarpa's work proved particularly respectful of the setting — both cultural and physical — in which he was operating. Instead of viewing the water as a problem, he chose to consider it as a resource, an opportunity, a source of inspiration. Rather than keeping the water from entering the building, Scarpa worked chiefly to allow it to flow easily out, and to make the building usable even during high water, by raising the floors affected by its presence as needed. The selection of appropriate materials reduced to an absolute minimum the problems caused by flooding. The water penetrates through a gate, where the main hall overlooks the canal, then runs along in a continuous stone channel — located along the walls, beginning in the entrance hall — without interfering with ease of circulation in the building. The walkway is thus transformed into a catwalk, and what was originally viewed as an obstacle becomes the theme of the project. One reaches the entrance, set askew from the axis of the main façade, by means of a bridge from the "campiello," or little square, near Santa Maria Formosa. The bridge too is an interesting piece of de-

sign: Scarpa makes it combine aspects of Japanism and pure Venetian style. The bridge's structure is made up of a steel centering that describes a taut arch, and rests upon two blocks of "pietra d'Istria," or Istrian stone, fastened to the foundations of the "campiello" and to the entrance to the palazzo. The centering is composed of two arches made of curved metal plate, separated by solid iron with a square cross section, joined at the central point. The supports of the railing, made with iron plates, welded and screwed together, bear a teak handrail that is reminiscent of naval architecture; the handrail is held up by round bars welded to an iron tube. To the left of the bridge,

two identical gates close off the arches of the portico that gives onto the canal. Each gate structure is articulated into two parts, the upper part being formed of solid round bars made of muntz metal, arranged vertically and set in iron housings; the lower part is made of iron structural shapes in varying thicknesses, arranged so as to form a pattern evocative of Oriental motifs. After crossing the bridge and the glass screen, one descends to the marble surface of the entrance-hall, a mosaic of polychrome marble taken from figurative motifs from the work of Paul Klee, also used at Castelvecchio. From the entrance-hall, one reaches the raised portico, destined for use in ex-

hibitions and conferences, passing by a full-height glass wall. The need to arrange here a number of features to give the environment some physical warmth prompted Scarpa to create a sculptural shell in "pietra d'Istria," with decorative bands in pure gold; this functional and sculptural form was set between the two rooms, and contains heating elements. In the main hall, which extends in length all the way to the courtyard, bands of "repen" subdivide a surface of washed concrete — which forms the flooring here and climbs a portion of the walls, to form

a high wainscoting. This flooring constitutes a modern interpretation of the traditional flooring made of courses of stone and cobble, found typically in the courtyards and "portegos" of the palazzi of Venice. Above the wainscoting, the walls are covered with two stacked bands of travertine of Rapolano, separated by a section of brass that is located at eye-level. This section, which also contains lighting equipment screened by opalescent glass, appears perfectly horizontal to the eye, because it represents the horizon line in terms of perspective and the symmetrical

axis of the two bands of travertine. On the right side of the hall we find a doorway made of travertine, which leads to the private room set aside for the speakers. This door has a shape that, when combined with the shape of the doorway, creates a distinctive pattern, sufficient to indicate its presence without interfering with the uniform texture of the travertine. The portico opens onto the garden, which Scarpa raised in order to establish a closer link to the view of those who are seated inside. This garden, too, consititutes a transposition of the traditional Venetian garden, which Scarpa interprets by emphasizing the regional flavor of the architecture. The water takes part, here once again, in a flowing interplay: a little basin made of off-purple Apuan marble catches the water as it drips from a small pipe, causing it to fill a series of little hollows, following a labyrinthine route, before spilling the water into a deep rivulet, where a number of waterlilies grow. On the far end of the little basin a small waterfall pours forth the water, so that the birds that live in the garden can drink; nearby is a long-dried-out well-curb.

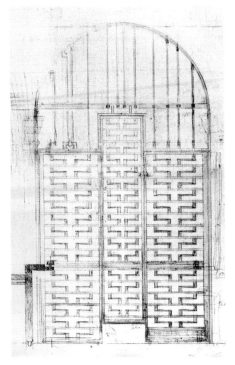

23

Gavina Showroom (now Simon)
1961-63
Bologna, Via Altabella
Telephone 39.51.269980

The store is located on the ground floor of a house in Bologna; originally there was a hardware store in this location. Scarpa was asked to reshape the chaotic space of the store — broken up by load-bearing walls — into a display area in line with the wishes of the clients. First of all, he marked off the boundaries of the store by placing a large sign on the façade. This façade is a cement slab, worked in bands with different sizes of chisels, subdivided into sections by bands with gold-leaf, and punctuated by three openings: a double circle, a single circle, and — in the middle — the entrance, the corners of which are underscored, as it were, by brass slots. The display windows, with glass flush to the surface, are supported by bosses in bronze and cast-iron. Scarpa always lavishes particular attention upon thresholds: the theme of a passage from one place to another is always an inexhaustible source of inventions. One cannot talk about architecture until there is an enclosure, a boundary that separates two structures: therefore, the awareness of crossing a threshold is a very important factor. On this occasion, Scarpa designed a little entrance-hall, closed off by an elegant gate, of modest size: it sets aside and invites one in, it does not close off the interior. After crossing through a little ambulatory that was meant to contain a statue, one reaches a screen on the interior of the store. Here Scarpa arranged vertical structural elements, enlarged and made plastic, with chromatic features of the composition. The pillars are made of various ma-

terials: pounded cement, cobalt-colored stucco, and shiny white-lime, with a brown coat applied with silver leaf; the last pillar, made of lamin-board and black plastic laminate, presents two holes clear through it, repeating the theme of the double circle, in wood, and revealing the hollow interior and revealing the thickness of the coat-ing. Instead of reducing to a minimum the supports holding up each of the stories of the house, Scarpa exaggerates their size and puts them out of alignment. When treated in this way, they lose every reference to the tectonic function that they perform, finding in architec-ture their prime motivation. To the left of the en-trance, a composition with geometric panels made of wood, where the service door is located, is a counterbalance to the cement fountain up-on which the polychrome mosaic by Mario De Luigi in glass-enamel tiles is reflected.

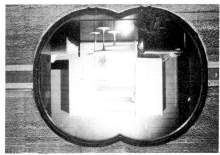

24

Museum of Revoltella
(with F. *Vattolo*)
1963-86
Trieste, Gallery of Modern Art, Viale
Diaz 27

Telephone 39.30.300938

Scarpa was commissioned in 1963 to undertake the remodeling of a block of the Borgo Giuseppino. The block was made up of three buildings: the Palazzo Revoltella, built by the architect Friedrich Hitzig, a student of Karl Friedrich Schinkel, and intended as a living museum; the Palazzo Brunner, adapted to a new function as a museum, and the little Palazzo Basevi, for the offices. The Palazzo Revoltella, the most interesting and the best preserved, was restored to be an exhibition, as it were, of itself; the Palazzo Brunner was emptied out in order to construct a complex spatial area, ideally suited for the ex-

hibition of works of art, endowed — through renovations of the roof — with terraces from which to admire the city; the Palazzo Basevi required minimal renovations. By maintaining the façades, it was possible to preserve the civic architecture of the block; inside the buildings a second shell was built, capable of supporting both the outer structure and the new, interior structure, so that it became possible to design a remarkable "raumplan" capable of expressing the typological content of the museum. An interior courtyard, created for the purpose of obtaining more natural light, produces a new, magically exterior space.

The work was completed, after the death of Scarpa, by the architects Franco Vattolo and Bartoli. Even though one senses the absence of the masterful touch that Carlo Scarpa's direct intervention would have brought about, the plan of the project is clear and powerful.

25

Wine Cellar at the Istituto Enologico, or Wine Institute

1964

Trent, San Michele all'Adige

Telephone 39.461.650108

The Istituto Enologico, or Wine Institute, is housed in the twentieth-century wing of an architectural complex that is located in the hills around San Michele all'Adige. Scarpa proposes here a wainscoting in bush-hammered concrete, forming an attachment between the building and the ground, running around the entire façade and radically modifying its appearance. This wainscoting hooks up with an inner glazed entrance, also in concrete, which marks the entrance, making it instinctively recognizable. The interior is enriched by the design of finishings and furnishings, as well as by a loft structure to increase the amount of space available for wine-tastings and the facilities of the wine cellar. Scarpa loved good wine, and often pointed out, while working on this project, that Alvar Aalto had been paid in wine for his work on the Maison Carré.

26

Renovation of the Balboni House
(with S. Los, G. Soccol)
1964-1974
Venice, Dorsoduro 12591, Ramo
Ambasciatori
Telephone 39.41.302742. Private residence, which
cannot be viewed from outside.

The renovation of this Venetian house was not completed by Scarpa. This is a two-story building, developed in length, the two shorter sides of which overlook a garden and the Grand Canal. Scarpa meant to take the greatest possible advantage of the light that is reflected from the water and the grass, modulating this light in a luminous longitudinal continuum. For this rea-

son, he made use of an open spiral staircase, created two facing elevations so as to link the various floors visually, and kept the colors very light. The staircase, in Lhasa marble, linked the living room overlooking the canal with the guest suite and, beyond that, with another living room that introduces one to the apartment — bedroom and facilities — of the lady of the

house. On the elevation overlooking the garden, two volumes were added, topped by a terrace, in order to enlarge the living room with bay windows and the kitchen. The house, which was completed by the architect Giovanni Soccol, represents an exceedingly interesting example of the renovation of an old Venetian house, located on a truly remarkable site.

27

Zentner House
(with S. Los, T. Senn)
1964-68
Zurich, Aurorastrasse
Private residence

The widow of Angelo Masieri remarried, taking as her second husband an engineer named Zentner, from Zurich; she commissioned Carlo Scarpa to renovate a home built in the Aurorastrasse in 1914. Limited by a very restrictive housing regulatory code, Scarpa went no further than to redesign the silhouettes of the three elevations, north, east, and west, while the southern elevation, which overlooks the garden, was articulated with jutting balconies and roofs. The ground attachment in worked concrete contrasted sharply with the amply glassed master floor, over which loomed a roof that shaded the façade in the summer. It is possible to note in this façade a number of features that reappear in later projects: the double windows of the Banca Popolare of Verona, the crown of the Museum of Revoltella, the horizontal mosaic of the Brion Tomb, and so on. This is where that transition begins that freed Scarpa's compositional system from the organic architecture of Frank Lloyd Wright. Particularly interesting and particularly well cared-for are the furnishings of this building: while still maintaining a continuity between the house and the garden, the interior space surprises the visitor with a new and different environment from the surrounding one. Again, this is a double shell: the outer shell, differentiated in its various orientations because it springs directly from the context, goes together with the interior one, which is welcoming and powerfully personalized.

28
De Benedetti-Bonaiuto House
(with F. Motterle, C. Maschietto, S. Los, E. Vittoria)
1965-72
Rome, Via Salaria
Private residence

This project was meant to include the restoration of a seventeenth-century Roman villa on the Via Salaria, and the construction of a small home in the adjacent park. First and foremost, the design centered on the construction of the house, which Scarpa had imagined as being like some sort of exquisite casing (a sort of Venetian tobacco-holder), set upon walls arranged to form open spaces in contact with the earth. This pavillion, raised from the ground so as to preserve the continuity of the garden, was meant to constitute a single great space — like in the houses designed by Mies van der Rohe — articulated into spaces, but still continuous. Scarpa worked continuously to refine the curves of this pavilion, made by combining circular arches, so as to attain a design that was in some way reminiscent of the architecture of Borromini. The structure that served to hold up the roof was meant to interfere as little as possible with the organization of the plan. Scarpa wished to resolve this problem with slender cylindrical columns joined in steel. Intended for an elderly person, the mother of a lawyer named De Benedetti, this simple house was meant to extend over a single level, so that the entrance way was also an inclined ramp running through the trees. The entire composition is based on the contrast between the pavilion — which, evoking a Roman baroque, is resolved entirely along enveloping curvilinear outlines — and the walls that supported it, in compliance with a De Stijl order.

29

Design for the Entrance to the University Institute of Architecture
(with S. Los)
1966, 1969, 1972
Venice, Santa Croce 191, Tolentini
Telephone 39.41.5297711

During the restoration of the convent of the Tolentini, where the Istituto Universitario di Architettura (University Institute of Architecture) of Venice is now located, a door was found, made of "pietra d'Istria"; plans were made to use it as an entrance to the school from the "campo," or square. When Scarpa was commissioned to do a renovation of the door, however, he never considered this "natural" use of the door. He did not intend to use the door for its original purpose — i.e., to pass through

it — but meant rather to display it, as if it were an artifact to be put on exhibition in a museum, and therefore for another, more complex, function. Having chosen this route, Scarpa activated the symbolic content of the door, multiplying the references and inserting it into a complex interplay of context and reminiscence that loaded it with meanings, as he had so often done in the past for artworks on display in mu-

seums. The wall which was supposed to enclose the little Campo dei Tolentini that stood before the entrance to the Department was also rejected decisively by Scarpa; in the solution that he proposed instead, the tectonic function was separated from the architectural function. The wall protected the little courtyard from outside, operating an enclosure, but from the interior it practically disappeared, becoming nothing more than a modelled flooring. For this entrance, Scarpa developed three designs. The first was developed in 1966, when Scarpa's studio was inside the school. The second developed and modified the first design in 1972; this received official zoning approval for construction, in the very years when Scarpa was the director of the institute. When I was commissioned to construct this project, on which I had worked from the beginning, I decided to build the

second design, because it was more complete, and less subject to the interpretative difficulties that an incomplete design can cause. The courtyard was not enclosed by a wall, but paved and raised, as so often is the case with Venetian "campi." The exterior edge of the pavement reveals the layers of which it is formed. These are two juxtaposed planes that curve from the center toward the sides of the itinerary. The inclination of the wall was further reduced and brought closer to the horizontal; the terracotta covering made it possible to use this pavement to sit and chat, as was the case in the courtyard before the renovation. The wall on the left, like a sign, supported a gate as well as a jutting canopy that protected those standing in front of the entrance from the elements. The canopy was made up of two stretched concrete sheets, one parallel and the other perpendicular to the inclined planes of the facing wall.

The ancient door was laid in a basin of water, the bottom of which was enlivened by steps that ran entirely around it, to form the elevation of an underwater landscape. The gate forms a sort of skewed balance, hanging by one wheel. On the one hand is a heavy slab of "pietra d'Istria," upon which is engraved a phrase from the work of Giambattista Vico, "verum ipsum factum," while on the other is the part that closes the entrance. A second wheel prevents the gate from overbalancing, and controls its movements. The door thus becomes a metaphor of the act of entering, intentionally abstracted from the role assigned it by functionalism. It is a lesson of architecture, given by using the same language in a critical manner.

30

Renovation of the Monument to the Female Resistance Fighter by Augusto Murer
(with S. Los)
1968
Venice, Giardini di Castello

Augusto Murer won a competition for the Monument to the Female Resistance Fighter, after a bomb destroyed the terracotta sculpture by Leoncilli. Murer had imagined a body reclining on the ground, marked by deep shadows; Scarpa thought that the only way to observe it from above was to see it from the quayside, arranging it upon the water. He imagined a floating caisson, that the sea would gently rock, to pre-vent the statue being engulfed at high tide. Around it, he designed a series of large rough square steps made of concrete and "pietra d'Is-tria," across which one could observe the stat-ue from a number of different points of view. A legend, lastly, would recall that the statue was dedicated to the Female Resistance Fighter. Scarpa, however, had not counted on the Port Oversight Commission, which insisted on hav-ing poles with spotlights; nor had he counted on the City Council, which insisted on installing a parapet, to limit access to the step-blocks, and which refused to repair the caisson, which was twisted loose by a particularly high tide; and last-ly, the pollution of the lagoon, which fetched up flotsam in amongst the square blocks.

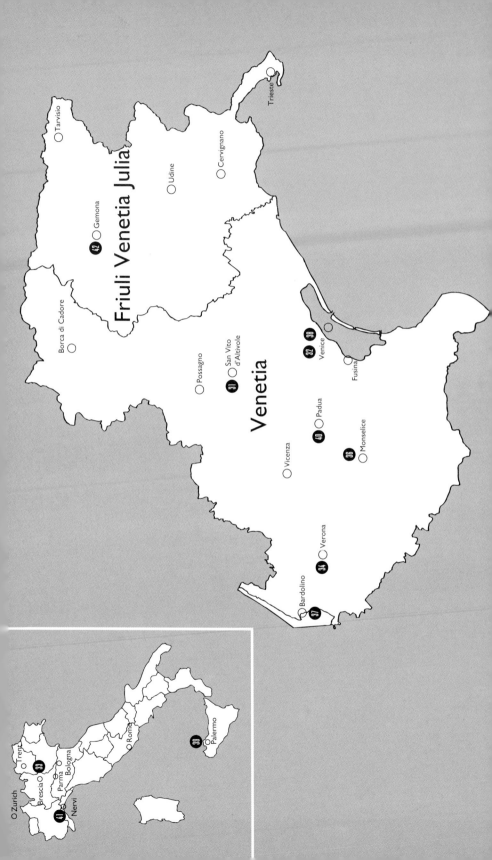

Trieste

Tarvisio

Cervignano

Friuli Venetia Julia

Udine

Gemona

42

Borca di Cadore

Possagno

San Vito d'Altivole

31

Venice

38

37

Fusina

Venetia

Padua

40

Monselice

36

Vicenza

Verona

34

Bardolino

37

Zurich

Trent

33

Bologna

Rome

Parma

Palermo

Brescia

39

Nervi

41

The rediscovered identity in the years of maturity

Scarpa felt in this period — with a tragic and final interruption during his trip to Japan — a strong sense of solitude; he felt the responsibility that attached to his personal contribution to the discipline of architecture, and his projects became increasingly spare and essential. Following his survey and tour of the architecture of Frank Lloyd Wright in the United States, Scarpa grasped just how radically different Wright's compositional research had been. The Brion tomb represents a culmination of the past experience — a sort of grammar of Scarpa's architecture — which ended one stage of research and began another. In the projects of these years, the classical matrix of Scarpa's compositional system became increasingly evident, along with the presence of a syntactical organization that withstood the polemical sideshows of each passing avant-garde. Though it appears exceedingly vulnerable, in actuality Scarpa's architecture is built to last: it is meant to establish a continuity between the past and the future and for that reason remains extraneous to the obsessive claims of the Zeitgeist, or spirit of the times. His references to classical order, which surfaces in the compositions of these later years, allow us to understand to what great degree this aspect, rather than constituting a hindrance, actually opened to his design new figurative potential and allowed him freedom that he could not have enjoyed otherwise. The manner of Scarpa — which many architects attempt to pursue — is that found primarily in the works of the second period, not those of the third, which are more difficult to understand and imitate. On many occasions, Scarpa pointed out that he was pursuing an architecture made of nothing, as if it were possible to attain in architecture that state of lightness that Italo Calvino was pursuing in literature.

31

Brion Monumental Tomb
(with G. *Pietropoli*, C. *Maschietto*)
1969-78
San Vito d'Altivole (Treviso), Cemetery
"A person had died, in Italy, and his family wished to commemorate the life of a man who had made his way up from the street, or as we say, from the 'mess-kit,' meaning, from the ranks; a man who had become important through his work. [...] I would have been completely satisfied with a hundred square meters to work in, but instead there were twenty-two hundred square meters. The owner certainly

had to build an enclosure wall! [...] So I built what you have seen. I decided to put the tomb here, the sarcophagi, one might say. For the tomb, a place in the glorious sunlight, and so here: panoramic vision. The deceased had asked to be near the earth, because he had been born in this place. And so I decided to build a little arch, which I shall call the 'arcosolium' ('arcosolium' is a Latin term used by the early Christians). In the catacombs, important personages or martyrs were buried in a more expensive manner, which was referred to as the 'arcosolium': it was nothing more than a simple arch, like this. It is lovely that two people who loved each other during their lives on earth should bend one toward the other to exchange greetings in death. They could not have been erect because that is the position of soldiers. This became an arch, a bridge: a bridge made of reinforced concrete, an arch made of reinforced concrete would have remained a bridge; in order to eliminate this sensation of a bridge, it was necessary to decorate it, to paint the vault. Instead I used a mosaic, which is in the Venetian tradition, interpreted in my own manner, which is a different manner. The great lane of cypress trees which leads to the cemetery is in the Italian tradition: it is a journey, or course. Architects are full of journeys. This course is called 'propylaeum'; it means door in Greek, entrance, this is the portico. One begins from here: these two eyes are the vision. For this purpose, the land was too extensive, in the meantime it has become [...] meadowland. In order to justify the enormous space, I thought that it might

be useful to have a little temple to make it more funereal, funeral is such a horrible word! Still too big; so then we raised the terrain so that I could see out. From here I can see out and from outside no one can see in. And so: tomb, family members, relatives, little temple, altar. From the town, one arrives through a special entrance, the church, the funeral, then the town cemetery, the chapel: this belongs to everyone, the land belongs to the state. The family has only the right to be buried. Here, a private lane leading to a little pavilion on the water, the only private object: this, in brief, is all. The place of the dead has the feeling of a garden — for that matter the great American cemeteries of the nineteenth century in Chicago are so many great parks. This is not the cemetery of Napoleon — terrible! One can go there by car: there are some lovely tombs, some of them designed by Sullivan. Now the cemeteries are made of piles of shoe-boxes, stacked mechanically. [...] I wanted, however, to render the natural sense of the concept of water and field, water and earth: water is the source of life." (from P. Duboy,

"Scarpa/Matisse: cruciverba," in F. Dal Co, G. Mazzariol (editors), *Carlo Scarpa. Opera Completa*, Milan, Electa, 1984, pgg. 170-171).

This description by Carlo Scarpa, reproduced verbatim, not only explains the motivations and preferences of the architect, but also recalls — for those who knew him — his ironic manner of explaining architecture.

His lessons were friendly chats, entirely free of any note of the academic. The Brion Tomb was designed while student protests were raging in the universities of Italy, architecture had been entirely forgotten because it was not very important politically, Scarpa was the head of a school that at that time no one else was interested in directing. And yet, in his gentle way, he managed to resist the ever-present hectoring and aggressivity, and designed a monument that testifies to the independence of architecture in the face of any and all ideological instrumentalization. This monument, which was so roundly criticized when it was first built, represents a sort of treatise that embodies, in architectural terms, his theoretical approach.

The land that contains that monument forms an L shape around two sides of the cemetery of San Vito d'Altivole, not far from Asolo. An inclined wall leaning inward marks off the space, indicating three important sites: the pond with the pavilion in the water, the "arcosolium" in the corner, and the chapel. There are two entrances, one directly from the exterior, toward the chapel, the other from the cemetery at the end of the central lane.

Through this second entrance, through which we shall pass — what Scarpa, recalling the Acropolis, liked to call the "propylaeum" — one reached a "portico," from which one can see the garden, through the two circles intersecting with the mosaic cornice. On the right of someone entering is the only private place, made inaccessible to visitors, a pavilion for meditation at the center of a pond. The movement of the glass door which closes off the passageway takes place through counterweights and pulleys which can be seen from the outside. In the pond, amongst the waterlilies, is an emblem: the labyrinth-cross.

32

Masieri Memorial
(with C. Maschietto, F. Semi)
1970-83
Venice, Dorsoduro 3900
Telephone 39.41.5226875

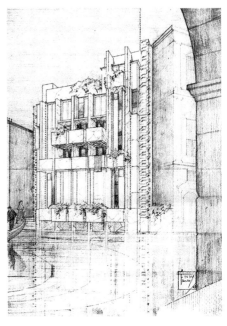

The history of the design of the building for the Masieri Foundation, which currently operates as a Gallery of Architecture, is a long one. It began in the years in which Carlo Scarpa was first working with a young Friulian architect, Angelo Masieri, with whom he shared the belief that the new architecture should follow the teachings of Frank Lloyd Wright. A number of the projects of those years — the bank of Tarvisio, the villa at Cervignano, and so on — bear the marks of a shared type of research, designed to explore that new spatial configuration that denotes organic architecture. During travel in the United States, Angelo Masieri, who was touring the buildings by Wright, was, tragically, killed in a

96

car crash in 1952. To commemorate their son, who had never been able to meet F.L. Wright, his parents asked the great American architect to design a building to be constructed in Venice on the Grand Canal, where they owned a small structure; the building was to serve as office space for a foundation run by the Istituto Universitario di Architettura di Venezia. Triggered by the project that Wright had developed for Venice, very fierce debates erupted, the result of which was unfortunate for the city, which thus lost the opportunity to establish a new and major project of contemporary architecture among the projects that so distinguish it. Indeed, no one had the courage to take the responsibility to allow the construction of that project, although some of the more forward-looking individuals in the city's architectural culture did

take a stand. Thus, after the building commission rejected the project in 1954, Carlo Scarpa jealously preserved the plans by Wright, hoping for better times. These plans were finally published in an issue of the journal *Metron* dedicated to Angelo Masieri. In 1962, the Masieri Foundation commissioned Valeriano Pastor to develop a new project, limited by very precise parameters of architectural conservation of the existing buildings; this project was never completed. It therefore fell to Scarpa to develop a renovation of the building as a "Casa dello Studente," or student union facility. Between 1968 and 1969, Scarpa developed a number of proposed projects, which encountered difficulties in the approval process, especially in the façade overlooking the Grand Canal. Then, one day, in a drawing by Canaletto, Scarpa found the version of the façade with two chimneys that had preceded the existing façade. He suggested, with the assistance of an engineer named Maschietto, a steel framework totally independent of the shell façade, intended to reduce to a minimum the thickness of the floors; this framework supported the façade while remaining visibly detached from it.

The project was finally approved in 1973, after the various complications and obstacles that characterized its entire complex existence. Following Scarpa's death, the project remained partially completed, in a roughed-out state, and was finally carried on by the engineer Maschietto and the architect Semi, who completed it in 1983.

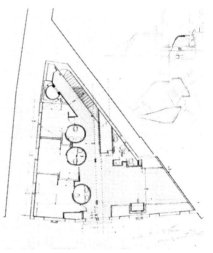

33
Museum of Arms at the Castello
(with F. *Rovetta*)
1971
Brescia, Castello (Castle)
Telephone 39.30.44176

The city government of Brescia commissioned Scarpa in 1971 to oversee the restoration of the museum (Scarpa asked to work with Rovetta); the government had already carried out a number of projects in the Sixties, under the supervision of the technical office. The project faced two fundamental issues: the relationship with the existing monumental structures, which had not been thoroughly studied, and the interaction with the previously completed restoration work. Scarpa imagined an itinerary punctuated by a series of events that were meant to orient the way in which one might "read" the stratified architectural "texts" that constitute the monumental complex of the castle of Brescia. Through the process of restoring the castle, to convert it into a museum, Scarpa made it eloquent and displayed it, as if it were part of the museum itself. During the fine-tuning of this project, to deal with considerations raised by the Archeological Commission, Scarpa made that tragic voyage to Japan during which he lost his life. When work resumed, Rovetta was supported by Arrigo Rudi; together they attempted to preserve the substance of Scarpa's original project, reducing to a minimum the modifications required in its construction.

34

Rehabilitation of the Central Headquarters and Annexes of the Banca Popolare di Verona
(with A. Rudi)
1973-81
Verona, Piazza Nogara 2
Telephone 39.45.8675111

The new headquarters of the Banca Popolare di Verona stands on the site of two buildings demolished for this purpose and next to the existing headquarters, which are still in use.

The project underwent a great deal of variation and change, due to new considerations brought up by the clients, or due to the architect's rethinking. Scarpa's work consisted of continually redesigning the building, and submitting his designs to a critical oversight review, that led to modifications, often minuscule, nearly undetectable changes. Those changes constituted the "fine-tuning" work that helped to orient, through tiny adjustments, the composition of the project. Like the face of a beautiful woman — Scarpa would say — which would lose its allure, its harmony, if we were to shift a single detail or proportion by even the smallest degree.

The basic themes of the project remained constant. A façade that was independent, and placed upon the building, composed with the classic tripartite structure: attachment on the ground floor, central body, and crowning level. The stone of the attachment on the ground floor ends in a moulding; the central body presents a stratification of stories such that the openings allow one to see the glass behind; the continuous loggia on the last floor allows the jutting

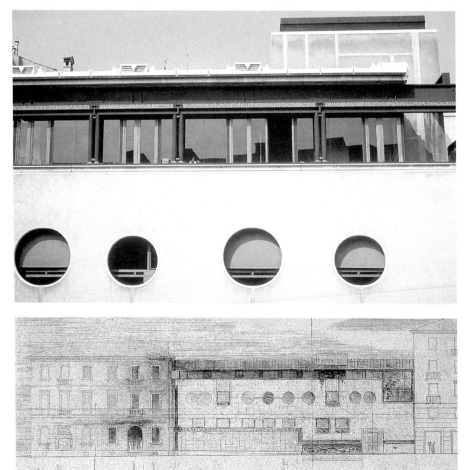

roof to project. At first, the rear façade was distinct from the main façade: it was treated with continuous horizontal bands, though it later took on the same fundamental features as the main façade. The plan is organized upon two axes that are not perfectly orthogonal. The skew, less than two degrees, was dictated by the placement and shape of the existing buildings: the enclosure wall of the old headquarters toward the new building, and the layout of the buildings facing Piazza Nogara. Rather than winding up with a trapezoid on either side, Scarpa chose to adopt a grid that was not perfectly orthogonal, to which he adapted the floors, the false ceilings, the steps of the staircases, and so forth. Upon Scarpa's death in November of 1978, the building had been roughly finished in all of its parts, and the two façades overlooking the piazza and the courtyard had been entirely completed, while much of the material needed for the interior finishings had been ordered. Rudi, who had overseen the project in all of its phases and the construction up to this point, undertook to finish the work he had begun, a commitment that he fulfilled quite well, adding to the other projects this major contribution by Scarpa to the fields of civic architecture and the architecture of office buildings. The façade, which is one of the most interesting elements in this project, presents openings with respect to which the glass planes are recessed or set forward. This is a fundamental motif, which can be found as well in the grid of the casements in sanded oakwood and in the bay windows that jut from the façade like so many glass display cases. The round openings are designed by juxtaposing arches and two narrowly placed centers, a mechanism that Scarpa suggested in order to make the circle more dynamic. Variants on this motif are two entwined circles, and the circular segment. The openings are cut out of the wall made of "cocciopesto" plaster (lime mixed with fragments of crockery), made by assembling five blocks of "botticino" marble, joined one to the other. On the exterior, the edge is rounded flush with the plaster, so as to make the form stand out even more sharply against the background. In the lower section, a narrow block of red Verona marble, which continues downward, contains the water runoff.

Other openings are cut into the base, in a large monolithic slab of "botticino" marble, with a design that is reminiscent of the enclosure made of marble and bronze, executed at Orsanmichele in Florence in 1366; the design is also not totally extraneous to Japanese designs. Every opening is rounded off on the interior, forming a diamond-point motif that allows the light to scatter and spread in a superior fashion. Because of the strong backlighting on the interior, one perceives a design that is the reverse of what is seen from outside. The façade ter-

minates with a cornice made of "botticino" marble, shaped with a stepped motif that allows Scarpa to evoke the motifs of classical architecture. The cornice hearkens back to the tradition of crowning structures on Venetian palazzi: in particular, the jutting surfaces, which receive intense sunlight, are inspired by the coping of the Fondaco dei Turchi. The denticulate moulding made of red Verona marble reappears in the bands on the façades, in correspondence with the windows, and on the interior, in the main stairwell. The façade ends with the window sills of the highest floor, as if the flat roof of the bank were just suspended in air; in the loggia above it, the materials change: supports and architraves made of metal, a frieze in colored mosaic. The long ribbon of the architrave, formed by two I-beams of different size, fastened one to the other with "fazzoletti" (slabs) and bolts, is supported at regular intervals upon pairs of joined small columns made of iron pipes. The columns are equipped with an annulet that serves as a continuous feature, joining up at the top with the architrave, at the bottom with the base. For items that must be produced on a lathe — if they need not support excessive weight — the normal alloy of brass-copper-zinc is too pasty, and so use was made of muntz metal, still a brass alloy in which the high percentage of zinc increases the rigidity and the fragility. Atop each pair of slender columns, in the dark

iron, gleams a little block of muntz metal, with the symbol of the joined circles; the links between the columns at the top and bottom are made of the same metal.

On the interior of the building, there are polygonal-sections columns made of reinforced concrete, the very tall cylindrical base in metal is fastened to the flooring with a bronze plate, and the capital is made of a small gilt annulet.

These columns constitute the regulatory elements of the interior space, otherwise punctuated by different features on each floor. The spatial continuity is ensured by a free arrangement of the walls, and with openings that link the different floors. The flooring and the skirting boards are made of "Clauzetto" marble; the ceilings — appropriately subdivided by iron sections that form panels — are made of Venetian stucco, colored and shiny. In the work spaces, the floors are made with large sqares of carpeting simply laid down, due to the requirements of plant engineering: under the panels of carpeting, in fact, are housed the ducts of the electrical system, which can be opened for inspection. The ceilings are made with sound-absorbing metal laths with tiny perforations. The walls are made of satinized lime plaster. The glass exterior rear stairway has a structure made of plaster-coated reinforced cement with a mixture of lime and powdered marble, The interior is constituted by a "gage" of steel pipes with corner joints in bronze. The steps of the staircase are made of high-resistance cement cast in a grid of iron plates. Other connecting features are characterized by rounded, colorful, shiny shells. Of particular interest in this connection is the employees' staircase, which links the various floors, the mezzanine, the basement and sub-basement; it is made up of two parallel ramps that are, however, arranged so as to obtain a vertical spatial continuity. The edges are protected with brass plates, the steps are made of "Clauzetto" marble, various surfaces are finished in shiny Venetian stucco, green and purple. The courtyard, where Scarpa designed a garden in the shape of an exedra, is crossed by a walkway about twenty meters in length; its metal structure is covered by shelter of curved plywood, coated with copper leaf. A support in the center separates the band into two spaces, where there is an adjustment between the heights of the two linked buildings. The façade of this bank represents a remarkable example of Scarpa's ability to insert a new building into the historical urban fabric, without a camouflaging historicism, but still in lively debate with the context.

35
Borgo House
(with G. Pietropoli)
1974
Vicenza, Via del Quartiere
It can be viewed from outside.

Scarpa accepted this commision for a residential building in Vicenza, after a previous project done by an engineer named Guiotto had failed to receive a building permit. Scarpa's great mastery at composition allowed him to move with agility among the endless array of restrictions imposed by the building code. The plan is interesting: part of the building runs along the road, presenting its façade to the city, while the other works its way into the garden. The section closest to the ground has a portico, in order to reveal the park behind it, but the entrance was marked by a second, low façade made of worked concrete. The elevations feature an intelligent interpretation of the Venetian theme of horizontal bands between the windows, and a clever haphazard distribution of the windows that run between the stringcourses.

36
Exterior Layout of the Villa Palazzetto
1974-75
Monselice (Padua), Via Palazzetto 1,
Businaro house
Telephone 39.429.72106

Completed in part, Scarpa's project called for a stairway that led directly from the entrance courtyard to the master floor of the villa. This is a remarkable interpretation of the traditional paved courts of the villas and farms, modelled through a series of slightly inclined, triangular planes, with a pattern that Scarpa reused in the terrace of the Ottolenghi house in Bardolino and in the final design for the entrance to the Campo dei Tolentini. There are other details worth examining in this villa, where a friend of the architect lives, such as a pergola, a brick and white-cement floor, the front door, a wooden gate, and so on. From the compositional system of Frank Lloyd Wright, Scarpa had by now gone on to work in an architectural syntax that sprang directly from the cities and villas of the Veneto.

37

Ottolenghi House
(with G. Tommasi, C. Maschietto, G. Pietropoli)
1974-79
Mure di Bardolino (Verona)

Telephone 39.45.7210478. Private residence, which cannot be viewed from outside.

In 1974, a lawyer named Ottolenghi commissioned Carlo Scarpa to build a house on Lake Garda, in the village of Mure, near Bardolino. The town zoning plan no longer permitted the building of houses fully above ground, and this consideration was transformed from a limitation to a contributing factor in the configuration of the final design. The solution was prompted precisely by the provocation of this zoning regulation: a partly underground building, organized around nine columns that acted as poles of attraction in the organization of the interior of the house. Many variations were made during the life of the project, and they were documented by Tommasi who — following Scarpa's death — decided to record them faithfully in a drawing that updated the original plans. There are, moreover, numerous studio drawings that tell us much about Scarpa's method of design, based on the idea of drawings as fundamental cognitive tools, as tools of research and analysis. The volume of the villa, not easily visible from a distance, merges — due to its unusual shape — with the natural setting in which it is contained. The design of the roof makes it "a bit of rough ground upon which it is also possible to walk" (Scarpa). The construction, made of reinforced cement, presents a roof formed of inclined planes, lined with ter-

racotta on the exterior, and with shiny black stucco on the interior. The roof was supposed to mirror the exterior landscape between the columns, as if the principle of the trilith could no longer be applied in its classic rigor, but only evoked and referred to. The columns refer to a plan with a covered courtyard, of which they constitute a deformation. The building takes air and light from a walkway, called the "calle," which separates it from the retaining wall

which was created by the meeting of two curved surfaces, one of them conical, the other obtained "by joining — as G. Tommasi put it — a straight-edged segment to a circumferential arch with straight generatrices." Fundamental features in the development of the design were the large rustic columns, made of large rocks alternating with stones and concrete. The treatment of the stone, according to the concept of Scarpa, should have been done on site, on the semi-complete structure, but it proved technically impossible to bushhammer stone and concrete at the same time. At first, a local stone, the "biancone di prun," was chosen and used; it was later decided to add a number of courses of "pietra di Trani," with a view to obtaining a more refined chromatic equilibrium. It has been mentioned that very similar pillars — at least in the proportions and construction technique, if not in the materials — can be found in the Romanesque church of San Severo, right in Bardolino. Scarpa, however, was not familiar with the interior of this church. The building that chiefly inspired Scarpa was the design by Frank Lloyd Wright for the Jester house in Palos Verdes, California, in 1938, even though the author, looking to the Venetian tradition, can hardly refrain from thinking of the Sarego villa by Andrea Palladio, also in the area around Verona. Large columns are found in other designs by Scarpa, such as the Villa Zoppas in Conegliano, the movie house of Valdobbiadene, the Roth House at Asolo; nonetheless, it was only in the Ottolenghi House that

they were actually built. The columns act as hinges for the various rooms, through polygonal grids, joined in unusual geometric arrangements. If we did not know the degree to which Scarpa rejected the fashions of art, we could attempt to identify a number of foreshadowings of deconstructivist compositional work. The interference between tradition and invention also generated the idea of the floor (cast in cement blended with grit and then polished), in which fragments of terracotta and colored stones are mixed as well, arranged to form a pattern that serves to guide and arrange the possible lines of breakage. Among the features that punctuate the itinerary of the interior, we should mention the fireplace by Mario De Luigi, the marble of Calacata, the polished colored stuccoes in the bathroom, by Eugenio De Luigi. The bathroom, in fact, was a central feature. Its shape derives from the joining of two sectioned circles, a recurring motif in Scarpa's architecture, and it acts as a spatial filter between the master bedroom and the large central hall of the living room. A one-way mirror was meant to allow one to observe without being observed, in Scarpa's plan. The spatial territory of someone in the bathroom continued into the entire bedroom; for those who are in the bedroom, on the other hand, the interior of the bathroom remained invisible. The furniture and interior decoration was also designed by Carlo Scarpa: among the items of furniture, in fact, we find pieces that he designed, the "Cornaro" sofa and the "Sarpi" table.

38

Entrance of the Department of Literature and Philosophy at the University of Venice
(with G. Pietropoli)
1976-78
Venice, Dorsoduro 1686, San Sebastiano
This entrance to the Department of Literature and Philosophy at San Sebastiano, like that of the University Institute of Architecture at the Tolentini, was built after Scarpa's death. This is a door set in the ground floor of the existing convent, with a design in the "pietra d'Istria" stone wall covering that focuses on an existing bas-relief. The project was supervised by a colleague of Scarpa's, the architect Pietropoli.

39

Palazzo Streri
(with R. Calandra)
1977-88
Palermo, Piazza Marina 66
Telephone 39.91.583177
Scarpa returned to Palermo where, many years

previous, he had planned the restoration of Palazzo Abatellis and the installation of a museum there; this time he had come to design the renovation of the fourteenth-century Palazzo Chiaromonte known as Palazzo Steri. The project called for the building to house the new offices of the rector of the University of Palermo, along with a small museum of the university's memorabilia. The entrance hall that overlooks Piazza Marina was rebuilt, articulating it into a sort of "architectural promenade" at varying levels. It is remarkable to note, in this context, how Scarpa, with minimal modifications, was able to emphasize and make eloquent the high ceilings of the halls, the doors onto the open arcade of the master floor, the grating-like casements of the biforate Gothic windows. The building is thus made visible, and in turn, able to see. It is the skilled modulation of light that renders relevant many of the features of the building or features arranged within the building, in the way that they are illuminated.

40

Altar and Flooring of the Church of Torresino

(with P. *Terrassan*)

1978

Padua, Piazza Torresino

Telephone 39.49.8758525 (parish priest)

In the central-plan church designed by Girolamo Frigimelica, which merges its Palladian compositional system with features taken from the Roman baroque, Scarpa designed the altar and the floor in which that altar is set. The church presents this central site, highly illuminated by a cupola supported by columns; for it, Scarpa designed a floor that echoes the texture of the carpet-floor at the entrance of the Querini Foundation and in the exterior covering of the sacellum at Castelvecchio. The flooring colors the light that the rhythm of the square tiles causes to reverberate around the altar. The altar, supported by twinned steel columns, is formed of a marble slab framed by a cornice in muntz metal, to which the supporting columns are attached by exquisite joints. The position of these supports presents a single axis of symmetry; the right and left sides are identical, but the forward side is different from the rear, as is appropriate to a table on one side of which stands the priest, while the faithful stand on the other side.

4|

Galli Family Tomb
(with M. *Pastorino*)
1978
Nervi (Genoa), Cemetery

The funerary aedicule designed by Scarpa for the Galli family and built after Scarpa's death is in the cemetery of Nervi at Sant'Ilario Alto. In the text that accompanied the design, Scarpa wrote: "The funerary aedicule for the Galli family represents an exceedingly spare structure, which fits well with the idea of the Absolute that is intrinsic and appropriate to death. "It is expressed in architectural terms with an elementary stone parallepiped, carved in such a way that light reverberates in and upon it. In this primary form, there is sunk a deep cavity that serves a dual purpose of introducing one to the funerary chamber and of blocking that chamber. "The funerary chamber, with its basement zone will be built in reinforced concrete. The outside surface will consist of a casing in worked white "botticino" marble, whose texture has been modified to give the surface a particular luminous vibrancy; the wall surface, seen in daylight, should give an impression of a particularly rough, uneven texture. "The movable stone that seals off the burial chamber is made of granite (flame-treated) so that the exterior surface can convey the idea of a stone corroded by time." This funerary monument marks the definitive transition for Scarpa, in terms of inspiration, from Frank Lloyd Wright to Adolf Loos.

42

Banca Popolare
(with L. *Gemin*, D. *Andretta*)
1978
Gemona (Udine), Piazza Garibaldi 9
Telephone 39.432.993711

This is yet another project completed after
Scarpa's death. This time, however, only a few
sketches, bare and preliminary, survive to document the great thought and extensive discussion that Scarpa had devoted to this building.
The principal themes emerge from those few
sketches: the theme of natural light for the interior, indicated by the large arches upon the
roof (found previously in the Banca Antoniana
in Monselice); the structuring of the gable

roof, marked at the juncture of the two pitches by the powerful jutting sign of the central balcony; and the definition of the volumetric whole in moderate dimensions and intentionally ordinary forms. Setting out from the design indications found in the sketches, Gemin developed the project as it was, finally, built.

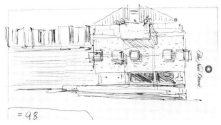

Some of the reproduction in the **Complete list of work** have been taken from the following:
Francesco Dal Co, Giuseppe Mazzariol, *Carlo Scarpa. The Complete Works*, Milan-London, Electa, 1984.
Paolo Ceccarelli, Sergio Los, Giuseppe Mazzariol, Italo Zannier, *Verum Ipsum Factum*, Venezia, Cluva, 1985.
Paolo Morello, *Palazzo Abatellis*, Treviso, Vianello, Libri, 1989.

Complete list of works

Site management for various religious buildings
Travettore di Rosà (Vicenza), Oderzo (Treviso), Santa Maria di Sala (Venice), Aviano (Udine)
1923-24

Annex to Villa Gioacchino Velluti
Dolo (Venice)
1924-25

Site management for new industrial installation and restoration of Palazzo Da Mula
Murano (Venice)
1925-26

Restoration of Villa Angelo Velo
(collaborator F. Pizzuto)
Fontaniva (Padua), Via Boschi
1926

Velo contractor's building-yard
(collaborator F. Pizzuto)
Fontaniva (Padua)
1926

Factory building with lodgings
(collaborator F. Pizzuto)
Fontaniva (Padua), Via Ponte
1926

Villa Giovanni Campagnolo
(collaborator F. Pizzuto)
Fontaniva (Padua)
1926

Villa Aldo Martinati
(collaborator F. Pizzuto)
Padua, Via Monte Grappa
1926

Studies for Teatro Sociale
1927

Artistic collaboration with the Murano glassworks Cappellin & Co.: objects at the IIIrd and IVth Exhibition of Decorative Arts
Monza (Milan)
1927-30

Showroom interiors for the Murano glassworks Cappellin & Co.
Florence, Lungarno Guicciardini
1928

Bedroom and diningroom of Vittorio Donà's house
Murano (Venice)
1929

Study for interior for the Murano glassworks Cappellin & Co.
Paris
1930

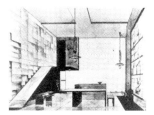

Numerous interior designs, some of them executed
Venice and Ravenna
1930 onward

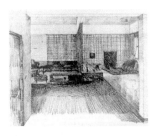

Interiors of Café Lavena
(with M. De Luigi)
Venice, Frezzeria
1931

Furnishings for livingroom in the Pelzel apartment
Murano (Venice)
1931

Furnishings for bar and children's bedroom in Ferruccio Asta apartment
(with M. De Luigi)
Venice
1931

Competition project for the Accademia bridge
(with A. and B. Piamonte)
Venice
1932

Sfriso silverware shop
(with M. De Luigi)
Venice, Campo San Tomà
1932

Project for Bassani house with two apartments
Cortina d'Ampezzo (Belluno)
1932

Collaboration on the fresco mosaic "Il bagno" at the XVIIIth Biennale
(with M. De Luigi)
Venice
1932

Artistic collaboration with the Venini firm for which he designed the booths at the VIth and VIIth Milan Triennale
1933-47

Competition project for the town plan of Mestre
(with M. De Luigi, A. and B. Piamonte)
Mestre (Venice)
1934

Project entered in a private competition for a passenger terminal at the Nicelli airport
(with G. Pellizzari, B. Piamonte)
Venice Lido
1934

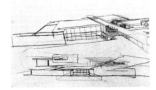

Project for the interiors of Nicelli airport
Venice Lido
1935

Projects for interiors, for the Arti Decorative Society
Venice
1935

Project for the interiors of the CPA
Rome
1935

Project for furnishings for a yacht belonging to Ferruccio Asta
Venice
1935

Studies for student residence, Ca' Foscari
Venice
1935-37

Restoration and layout of Ca' Foscari
Venice
1935-37

Furnishings of the private roulette room at the Casino
Venice Lido
1936

Venini booth at the VIth Milan Triennale
Milan
1936

Project for the interiors of M. house
Venice Lido
1937

Installation of the exhibition "Venetian Goldsmiths"
Venice, Loggetta del Sansovino
1937

Gino Sacerdoti apartment
Venice, San Gregorio
1937

Layout of Cinema Teatro Rossini
Venice
1937 ca.

Project for a station for the municipal ferry system on the lagoon (ACNIL)
(with M. De Luigi)
Venice Lido
1937

Interiors of the "Flavio" beauty parlor
Venice Lido
1939

Project for the restoration and conversion of a block of small apartments for Gino Sacerdoti
Venice, San Gregorio
1940

Tomb of Vettore Rizzo
Venice, San Michele
Cemetery
1940-41

Venini booth at the VIIth Milan Triennale
Milan
1940

Layout and interior design for the Hoffer house
Venice Lido
1940-50 ca.

Plan for "Il Cavallino" gallery of contemporary art
Venice, Riva degli Schiavoni
1941

Restoration of the apartment for Gino Sacerdoti
Venice, Santa Maria del Giglio
1941

Furnishing for the apartment of Arturo Martini
Venice, San Gregorio
1941

Bedroom and diningroom furniture for Gigi Scarpa
Venice
1941

Plan and interiors for the Pellizzari apartment
(with Pellizzari)
Venice, Santa Fosca
1942

Installation of the "Arturo Martini" exhibition,
(with M. De Luigi)
Venice, Castello Gardens, Biennale
1942

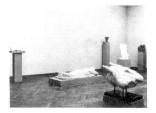

Project for the Grazioli house
San Pietro in Gu (Padua)
1943

Capovilla family tomb
Venice, San Michele Cemetery
1943-44

Studies for a new layout of the Gallerie dell'Accademia
(with V. Pastor)
Venice
1944

Interiors for the Tessiladriatica store
Venice, Campo Santi Apostoli
1944

Renovation of Bellotto apartment
Venice, Campo Santi Apostoli
1944

Layout of the Gallerie dell'Accademia
(with V. Pastor)
Venice
1945 onward

Project for a cinema with cafe and bar facilities
(with E. Mantese, De Toffoli)
Valdobbiadene (Treviso)
1946

Competition project for a master plan for the Lido
(with pupils, C. Maschietto)
Venice Lido
1947

Project for layout officies of the Transadriatica agency
Venice, San Marco
1947

Study for an apartment building
(with Iscra)
Padua, Piazza Spalato
1947

Premises of the Banca Cattolica del Veneto
(with A. Masieri)
Tarvisio (Udine), Via Roma
1947-48

Project for the Banca Cattolica del Veneto
(with A. Masieri)
Udine
1947-49

Giacomuzzi House
(with A. Masieri)
Udine
1947-50

Project for a branch of the Banca Cattolica del Veneto, entry in an invitational competition (second-prize winner)
(with A. Masieri)
Cervignano del Friuli (Udine)
1948

Project for a complex comprising bus station and office building to be integrated into Piazza Mazzini
Padua
1948

Project for parish church using prefabricated elements
Torre di Mosto (Venice)
1948

Project for a bridge
(with Ravà contractors, Venice)
Fontaniva di Brenta (Padua)
1948

Installations for the XXIVth Venice Biennale
Venice, Castello Gardens, Biennale
1948

Interior for the "First Exhibition of Film Tecnique"
Venice Lido, Temporary Cinema Pavilion
1948

Project for calculating machine booth
(with M. De Luigi)
Padua, Trade Fair
1948

Layout of the Pedrocchi Café
Padua
1948-50

Studies for the Hotel Bauer
Venice, San Moisé
1949

Project for apartment building
Feltre (Belluno)
1949

Preliminary design for a two-story building with two apartments
Maerne (Venice)
1949

Project for the Astra Cinema
San Donà di Piave (Venice)
1949

Interiors of the new premises of "Il Cavallino" contemporary art gallery
Venice, Frezzeria
1949

Booth for the press and cinema advertising
Venice Lido, Palazzo del Cinema, Lungomare Marconi (temporary cinema pavilion)
1949

Installations for the "Giovanni Bellini" exhibition
Venice, Doge's Palace
1949

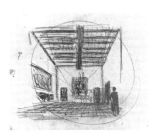

Installation of the exhibition "Survey of Contemporary Art"
Venice, Ala Napoleonica
1949

Studies for design of lobby and reception rooms at the Hotel Danieli
Venice, Riva degli Schiavoni
1949-50

Layout of a public telephone facility Telve
Venice, Ascensione
1950

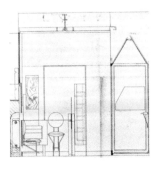

Layout and furnishings for Ferdinando Ongania's antique shop
Venice, Bocca di Piazza
1950

Project for a house for Mario Guarnieri
Venice Lido
1950

Interior of the "A la piavola de Franza" boutique
Venice, Bocca di Piazza
1950

Book pavilion
Venice, Castello Gardens, Biennale
1950

Installations for the XXVth Biennale
Venice, Castello Gardens, Biennale
1950

Installations for the exhibition "Posters of the Biennale"
Venice, Napoleonic wing
1950

Installations for the exhibition "Images of Work in Contemporary Painting"
Venice, Napoleonic wing
1950

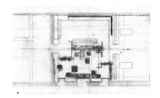

Installations for the "Exhibition of Cinema Books and Periodicals", XXVth Biennale
Venice Lido, Palazzo del Cinema, Lungomare Marconi
1950

Bortolotto house
(with A. Masieri)
Cervignano del Friuli
(Udine), via Udine
1950-52

Veritti tomb
(with A. Masieri)
Udine, San Vito Cemetery
1951

**Booth for the IXth Milan
Triennale**
Milan
1951

**Installations for the
exhibition "G.B.
Tiepolo"**
Venice, Castello Gardens,
1951

**Installations for the
XXVIth Biennale**
Venice, Castello Gardens,
Biennale
1952

**Project for organization
of the Contemporary Art
Archives of the Biennale**
Venice, Ca' Giustinian
1952

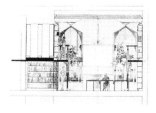

**Garden of the Guarnieri
house**
Venice Lido
1952

**Installations for the
exhibition "Toulouse
Lautrec"**
Venice, Napoleonic wing
1952

**Installations of an
exhibition for the
Istituto Nazionale di
Urbanistica conference
(INU)**
Venice, Ca' Giustinian
1952

**Installation of an
exhibition of historical
financial documents
from Siena**
Venice, Marciana library
1952

**Renovation of the
Ambrosini apartment**
Venice, Corte Zoia 240
1952-53

Project for Villa Zoppas
(with P. Celotto)
Conegliano (Treviso)
1953

**Layout of the historic
sections of the Correr
Museum**
Venice, Saint's Mark Square
1953

**Installation of the
exhibition "Antonello
da Messina and the
Quattrocento in Sicily"**
Messina, Palazzo del
Municipio
1953

**Restoration of Palazzo
Abatellis as the Galleria
Regionale di Sicilia**
(with R. Calandra)
Palermo, Via Alloro 4
1953-54

**Installation for the
exhibition "Ancient
Chinese Art"**
(with V. Pastor)
Venice, Ducal Palace
1954

**Installation for displays
in the first rooms of the
Uffizi gallery**
(with I. Gardella, G.
Michelucci)
Florence
1954-56

Venezuelan pavilion
(with C. Maschietto, V.
Pastor, G. D'Agaro,
Marchesin)
Venice, Castello Gardens,
Biennale
1954-56

**New layout of the "Aula
Magna" of Ca' Foscari**
(with V. Pastor, G.
D'Agaro)
Venice
1954-56

Competition project for a cultural center
(with G. D'Agaro, E. Detti, V. Pastor)
La Spezia
1955

Installation of Leonardo Leoncilli's statue "La partigiana"
(with V. Pastor)
Venice, Castello Gardens
1955

Interior design for the Manlio Capitolo civil court, Venice law court
(with V. Pastor)
Venice, San Polo, near Rialto Bridge
1955

Furnishings for a law office at Santa Maria Formosa and an apartment in the Calle degli Avvocati, both for the attorney Scatturin
(with V. Pastor)
Venice
1955

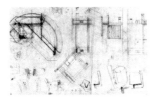

Interior design of the council chamber in the offices of the Amministrazione Provinciale
(with V. Pastor, G. D'Agaro),
Parma, Piazzale della Pace
1955-56

Extension of the Canova plaster cast gallery
(with V. Pastor)
Possagno (Treviso), Piazza Canova
1955-57

Veritti house
(with F. Marconi, C. Maschietto)
Udine, Viale Duodo
1955-61

Installation of "Piet Mondrian" exhibition
Rome, Valle Giulia modern art gallery
1956

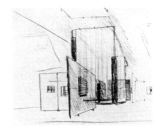

Competition for the Olivetti factory vacation colony
(with G. D'Agaro)
Brusson (Ivrea)
1956

Collaboration on a parish church
(with E. Detti)
Fiorenzuola (Piacenza)
1956

Restoration and reorganization of the Castelvecchio Museum
(with C. Maschietto, A. Rudi)
Verona, Castelvecchio
1956-64

Design for the Taddei house
Venice, Rio Terà dei Catecumeni
1957

Preliminary project for premises of La Rinascente department store
Catania, Via Etnea
1957

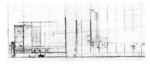

Layout of a camping-site at Fusina
Fusina (Venice)
1957

Olivetti showroom
(with G. D'Agaro, C. Maschietto)
Venice, Procuratie Vecchie
1957-58

Renovation of the painting gallery in the Correr Museum
(with V. Pastor, G. D'Agaro)
Venice, Saint's Mark Square
1957-60

Collaboration on plan for renovation of the drawings and prints collection in the Uffizi Gallery
(with E. Detti)
Florence
1957-60

Installation of the XXIXth Biennale
Venice, Castello Gardens, Biennale
1958

Installation for the exhibition "From Altichiero to Pisanello"
Verona, Castelvecchio Museum
1958

Study for a shop at Santa Maria del Giglio and scheme for a showroom at San Gregorio for the Salviati glassworks
Venice, San Gregorio
1958-60

Collaboration on a high school
(with C. Maschietto)
Chioggia (Venice)
1958-61

Collaboration on projects for Hotel Minerva, Florence, professional and commercial high school, Carrara, high school, Leghorn, law-office building, Massa, premises for the publishers La Nuova Italia, Florence
(with E. Detti)
1958-70

Second prize in the competition for a set of silver cutlery, on invitation from Reed & Barton
(with T. Scarpa)
Boston
1959

Church in the ENI village
(with E. Gellner)
Borca di Cadore (Belluno)
1959

Installation of the exhibition "Vitality in Art"
Venice, Palazzo Grassi
1959

Installation of the exhibition "Murano Glassware, 1860-1960"
(with A. Rudi)
Verona, Gran Guardia
1959

Study for the renovation of the Taddei apartment
Venice, Palazzo Morosini
1959

Plan for the D'Ambrogio apartment
Udine, Via Leopardi
1960

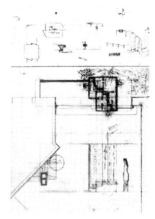

Zilio tomb
Udine, San Vito Cemetery
1960

Installation for the "Frank Lloyd Wright" exhibition, XIIth Milan Triennale
Milan
1960

Installation for the XXXth Biennale
Venice, Castello Gardens, Biennale
1960

Installation for the exhibition "The Sense of Color and the Rule of the Waters," in the Veneto pavilion at the "Italia '61" national exhibition
Turin
1961

Reorganization of the ground floor and courtyard of the Fondazione Querini Stampalia
(with C. Maschietto)
Venice, Campo Santa Maria Formosa
1961-63

Gavina (now Simon) showroom
Bologna, Via Altabella
1961-63

Installations for the XXXIst Biennale
Venice, Castello Gardens, Biennale
1962

Installation for the "Cima da Conegliano" exhibition
Treviso, Palazzo dei Trecento
1962

First project for renovation of the Italian pavilion at the Venice Biennale
(with T. Scarpa)
Venice
1962-63

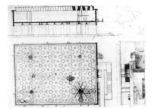

Plan for the Gallo house
Vicenza, Contrà Santa Croce
1962 onward

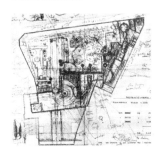

Project for renovation of the Scarpa apartment
Venice, Rio Marin
1963

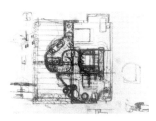

Project for the Secco house
(with G. Davanzo)
Treviso
1963-64

Project for the Cassina house
Ronco di Carimate (Como)
1963-64

Project for the reorganization of the Revoltella Museum
(with F. Vattolo)
Trieste, Galleria d'arte moderna, Viale Diaz
1963-86

Project for reconstruction of the Carlo Felice theater
(with L. Croce, M. Zavelani-Rossi, S. Los)
Genoa
1963 onward

Project for extension of the Albergo dei Duchi
(with S. Los)
Spoleto
1964

Cellars of the Enological Institute
San Michele all'Adige (Trent)
1964

Project for a permanent exhibition of Trentino craftsmanship
(with Boato, Ketmaier)
Trent
1964

Installation for the "Giacomo Manzù" exhibition
Venice, Napoleonic wing
1964

Installation for the XXXIInd Biennale
Venice, Castello Gardens, Biennale
1964

Second project for the renovation of the Italian pavilion at the Biennale
(with S. Los)
Venice, Castello Gardens, Biennale
1964-65

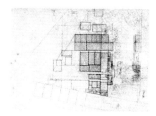

Zentner house
(with S. Los, T. Senn)
Zurich, Aurora Strasse
1964-68

Restoration of the Balboni apartment
(with Soccol, S. Los)
Venice, Ramo Ambasciatori
1964-74

Studies for the roof of the terrace of the Istituto universitario di architettura
(with S. Los)
Venice
1965 ca.

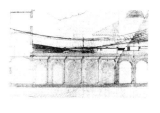

De Benedetti-Bonaiuto house
(with F. Motterle, C. Maschietto, S. Los, E. Vittoria)
Rome, Via Salaria
1965-72

Project for Piazza Duomo
Modena
1966

Project for competition for the reconstruction of the Art gallery
Munich
1966

Project for the entrance to the Istituto universitario di architettura
(with S. Los)
Venice, Campo dei Tolentini
1966

Design for the renovation of Palazzo Labia as premises of RAI
(with A. Scattolin, S. Los)
Venice
1966

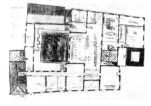

Installations for the XXXIIIrd Biennale, central pavilion
Venice, Castello Gardens, Biennale
1966

Project for Pier Carlo Santini's house
(with F. Motterle)
Lucca
1967

Installations for the " La Poesia" section of the Italian pavilion at "Expo67"
(with S. Los)
Montreal
1967

Installations for the exhibition "Arturo Martini"
(with L. Gemin, G. Davanzo)
Treviso, Santa Caterina
1967

Project for a monumental cemetery
Modena
1967-69

Installation design for a monument to the women of the Resistance by Augusto Murer
(with S. Los)
Venice, Castello Gardens
1968

Installations for the XXXIVth Biennale
(with P. Leone)
Venice, Castello Gardens, Biennale, central pavilion
1968

Project for an invitational competition to design an urban theater
Vicenza
1968-69

Studies for the lighting and layout of public gardens
Castelfranco (Treviso)
1969

Studies for an optician's store
Bolzano
1969

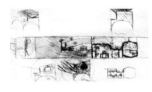

Installations for the exhibition "Florentine Frescoes"
London, Hayward Gallery
1969

Brion tomb
(with G. Pietropoli, C. Maschietto)
San Vito d'Altivole
(Treviso), Cemetery
1969-78

Installation for the exhibition "Drawings by Erich Mendelsohn"
Berkeley (USA),
University of California
1969

Project for an organ loft in the church of the Frari
(with G. Pietropoli)
Venice
1970

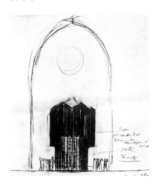

Project of country club
(with F. Motterle, G. Pietropoli)
Montecchio Maggiore,
Sant'Urbano, Costalta
(Vicenza)
1970

Installation of the "Giorgio Morandi" exhibition
London, Royal Academy of Arts
1970

Masieri Memorial
(with C. Maschietto, F. Semi)
Venice, Dorsoduro
1970-83

Studies for the Buonpensieri store
Bologna
1971

Design for the Roth house
Asolo (Treviso)
1971-72

Project for the Armory Museum at the Castle
(with F. Rovetta)
Brescia, Castello
1971

Project for the Lupi house
(with F. Motterle)
outskirts of Vicenza
1972

Installations for the exhibition "Masterpieces of Twentieth-Century Painting"
Venice, Ala Napoleonica
1972

Installations for the XXXVIth Biennale
Venice, Castello Gardens,
Biennale
1972

Studies for renovation of the Franchetti gallery
(with G. Pietropoli)
Venice, Ca' d'Oro,
Cannaregio
1972-73

Project for a book deposit and guest rooms of the Fondazione Querini Stampalia
(with F. Giuliani)
Venice
1973

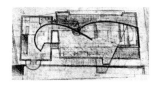

Project for the Fini restaurant
(with C. Maschietto, F. Motterle, F. Rovetta)
Modena
1973

Project for a renovation of the top floor of the museum of Villa Strozzi
Florence
1973

Consultation work for the installation of the Tancredi exhibition
Milan, Rotonda di Via Besana
1973

Installation for the exhibition "Ritratto di Venezia"
(with V. Pastor, U. Franzoi)
Venice, Napoleonic wing
1973

Installation for the exhibition "Le Corbusier the Purist and the Pessac Project"
(with F. Rovetta)
Venice, Fondazione Querini Stampalia, Campo Santa Maria Formosa
1973

Layout of the main premises and annexes of the Banca Popolare di Verona
(with A. Rudi)
Verona, Piazza Nogara
1973-81

Project for the Galleria nazionale d'Arte
(with F. Calandra, F. Lombardo)
Messina
1974

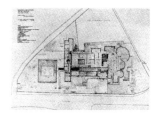

Borgo house
(with G. Pietropoli)
Vicenza, Via del Quartiere
1974

Installations for the exhibition "Venice and Byzantium"
(with U. Franzoi)
Venice, Ducal Palace
1974

Installation for the exhibition "Gino Rossi"
(with L. Gemin)
Treviso, Ca' da Noal
1974

Installation for the exhibition "Carlo Scarpa", in response to an invitation from the RIBA
(with A. Irvine, G. Pietropoli)
London, Heinz Gallery
1974

Installation for the exhibition "Carlo Scarpa"
(with F. Motterle, G. Pietropoli)
Vicenza, Domus Conestabilis
1974

Project for a monument to the victims of the massacre in Piazza della Loggia and commemorative columns for its second anniversary
(with F. Rovetta)
Brescia
1974-75

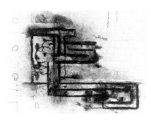

Project for the conversion of the convent of Santa Caterina into a museum
(with L. Gemin)
Treviso
1974-75

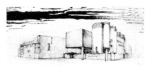

Project for the extension and restoration of Villa Matteazzi-Chiesa
(with F. Motterle)
Vicenza, Ponte Alto
1974-75

External renovation of Villa Palazzetto
(with C. Maschietto)
Monselice (Padua),
via Palazzetto
1974-75

Project for modification of the convent of San Sebastiano for the new premises of the Faculty of Literature and Philosophy of the University of Venice
(with G. Pietropoli)
Venice, San Sebastiano
1974-78

Ottolenghi house
(with G. Tommasi, C. Maschietto, G. Pietropoli)
Bardolino (Verona)
1974-79

Consultation on the new layout of the "Interior design club" showroom
Florence, Via delle Mantellate
1975

Layout of the main hall of the Istituto Universitario di Architettura
Venice, Dorsoduro
1975

Installation for the exhibition "Giuseppe Samonà. 50 years of Architectures"
(with F. Rovetta)
Venice, Palazzo Grassi
1975

Installation of the exhibition "Carlo Scarpa"
(with F. Rovetta, G. Tommasi)
Paris, Institut de l'Environnement
1975

Project for the extension of Villa Zileri dal Verme
(with F. Motterle)
Vicenza
1975-76

Project for restoration of the Urbinati house
Pesaro
1975-76

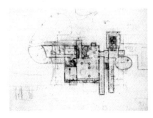

Progject for three vacation houses
(with Toyoda, Bagnoli, Zuliani)
Quero (Belluno)
1975-76

Project for protection and display of Roman remains
(with U. Franzoi)
Feltre (Belluno)
1975-78

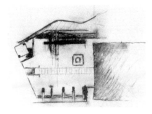

Project for the Picasso Museum
(with P. Duboy, P. Saddy, P. Rigoni)
Paris, Hôtel Salé
1976

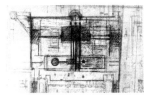

Project for condominium block
Lugo (Ravenna), Via Tellarini
1976

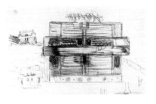

Consultation on the interior of the "Giglio" clothing store
Palermo
1976

Project for the Banca Antoniana
(with P. Rigoni)
Monselice (Padua)
1976-77

Studies for plan of the offices of the Regione Veneto
(with V. Pastor)
Venice, Procuratie Nuove
1976-77

Design of the new portal for the Faculty of Literature and Philosophy of the University of Venice
(with G. Pietropoli)
Venice, San Sebastiano
1976-78

New project for the entrance to the Istituto universitario di architettura (IIIrd draft)
Venice, Campo dei Tolentini
1977

Study for the church of Santa Maria delle Rose
(with G. Pietropoli)
Rovigo
1977

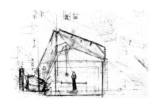

Project for the Benetton condominium
(with L. Gemin, C. Maschietto)
Treviso, Via IV novembre
1977

Project for a forniture showroom
Guastalla (Mantua)
1977

Palazzo Steri
(with R. Calandra)
Palermo, Piazza Marina
1977-88

Interior design of an apartment
Montecchio (Vicenza)
1977

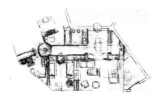

Consultation regarding improvements to the Roman villa
Verona, Palazzo Forti
1977

Installation of the exhibition "Alberto Viani"
Venice, Ca' Pesaro
1977

Project for the Mobilfiorente forniture factory
(with S. Bagnoli)
Scarperia (Florence)
1977-78

Project for the Alessi showroom
(with S. Bagnoli)
Bassano del Grappa (Vicenza)
1977-78

Zoppi apartment
(with G. Pietropoli, P. Terrassan)
Vicenza
1977-78

Banca Popolare
(L. Gemin, Andretta, from a project of C. Scarpa), Gemona (Udine), Piazza Garibaldi
1978

Project for the library of the Scuola Normale Superiore
(with P. Terrassan)
Pisa, Palazzo della Gherardesca
1978

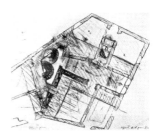

Preliminary studies for a large Villa, Al Saaud
(with Picco, Toyoda)
Ryadh (Saudi Arabia)
1978

Project for a house
Oneglia (Imperia), Via 9 novembre
1978

Altar and paving for the church of Torresino
(with P. Terrassan)
Padua, Piazza Torresino
1978

Tomb for the Galli family
(with M. Pastorino)
Genoa Nervi, cemetery
1978

Installation for the exhibition "Carlo Scarpa"
Madrid
1978

Installation for the exhibition "Mario Cavaglieri"
(with G. Pietropoli)
Rovigo, Accademia dei Concordi
1978

Bibliography

1932
ed., "Arredamento a Venezia di De Luigi e Scarpa", *La Casa Bella*, 55, pp. 34-37.

1938
E. SALVIATI, "Arte e industria vetraria muranese", *Architettura*, November.

1940
B. CAIZZI, "Umbau des Palazzo Foscari", *Das Werk*, 8.

1942
R. GIOLLI, "Alla Biennale di Venezia", *Costruzioni-Casabella*, 175, July, pp. 36-37.

1948
V. MOSCHINI, "La nuova sistemazione delle Gallerie di Venezia", *Bollettino d'arte del Ministero della P.I.*, 1, pp. 85-90.
G. PONTI, "Appunti alla regia della Biennale", *Domus*, 228, p. 1.

1950
ed., "Padiglione dei libri d'arte", *Metron*, in 38, pp. 17-20.

1952
ed., "Ufficio telefonico pubblico a Venezia", *Metron*, 45, pp. 41-46.

1953
R. LONGHI, "Frammento Siciliano", *Paragone*, 47, pp. 3-44.

1955
G. MAZZARIOL, "Opere di Carlo Scarpa", *L'architettura-c.s.*, 3, pp. 340-367.

1956
F. TENTORI, "Un padiglione di Carlo Scarpa alla Biennale di Venezia", *Casabella-continuità*, 212, pp. 19-30.
G. VIGNI, "Nouvelle installation de la Galleria Nazionale della Sicilia, Palerme", *Museum*, 4, pp. 201-214.
P. VIOLA, *Inaugurazione della sala del Consiglio*, catalogue, Parme.

1957
V. MOSCHINI, "Nuovi allestimenti e restauri alle Gallerie di Venezia", *Bollettino d'Arte del Ministero della P.I.*, 1, pp. 74-81.
R. SALVINI, "Il nuovo ordinamento della Galleria. Sistemazione di alcune sale della Galleria degli Uffizi (Gardella-Michelucci-Scarpa)", *Casabella-continuità*, 214, pp. 20-25.
B. ZEVI, "I premi nazionali d'architettura e urbanistica a Carlo Scarpa e Ludovico Quaroni", *L'architettura-c.s.*, 15, pp. 628-629.

1958
R. PEDIO, "Concorso per una colonia a Brusson", *L'architettura-c.s.*, 37, pp. 458 and 468-469.
F. TENTORI, "Progetti di Carlo Scarpa: casa Veritti a Udine e casa

Taddei a Venezia", *Casabella-continuità*, 222, pp. 15-20.
ed., "Ampliamento della Gipsoteca Canoviana a Possagno", *Casabella-continuità*, 222, pp. 8-14.

1959
M. BRAWNE, "Object on View", *The Architectural Review*, 753, pp. 242-253.
L. MAGAGNATO, "A Verona, il restauro di Castelvecchio", *Comunità*, 75, pp. 60-66.
C.L. RAGGHIANTI, "'La Crosera de piazza' di Carlo Scarpa", *Zodiac*, 4, pp. 128-147.
G. SCARPA, "Un negozio in Piazza S. Marco a Venezia", *L'architettura-c.s.*, 43, pp. 18-27.

1960
S. BETTINI, "L'architettura di Carlo Scarpa", *Zodiac*, 6, pp. 140-187.
G. MARIACHER, "L'allestimento della Quadreria Correr", *Bollettino d'Arte del Ministero della P.I.*, 2, pp. 4-15.
ed., "Il nuovo negozio Olivetti a Venezia", *Domus*, 362, pp. 8-14.
ed., "L'opera di Carlo Scarpa al Museo di Castelvecchio a Verona", *Domus*, 369, pp. 39-53.

1961
R. ALOI, "Casa Veritti a Udine", in *Ville nel mondo*, Milan, pp. 1-12.
G. MARIACHER, "La Quadreria Correr", *L'Oeil*, 76.

P.C. SANTINI, "'Italia '61'. La mostra delle regioni", Comunità, 90, pp. 10-19.
F. TENTORI, "Quindici anni di architettura", Casabella-continuità, 251, pp. 35-50.

1962
J. RYKWERT, "Sulla mostra di Cima a Treviso", Domus, 396.
P.C. SANTINI, "Un'opera distrutta di Carlo Scarpa", Zodiac, 9, pp. 146-161.
P.C. SANTINI, "Il nuovo negozio di Carlo Scarpa a Bologna", Zodiac, 10, pp. 169-181.
C. SCARPA, "Negozio a Bologna", Domus, 395, pp. 3-13.
ed., "L'opera di Carlo Scarpa in Palazzo Abatellis a Palermo – L'opera di Carlo Scarpa alla Quadreria Correr in Venezia", Domus, 388, pp. 17-34.

1964
G. MAZZARIOL, "Un'opera di Carlo Scarpa: il riordino di un antico palazzo veneziano", Zodiac, 13, pp. 26-59.
Scarpa, Carlo, entry in Encyclopedia of Modern Architecture, New York.

1965
M. BOTTERO, "Carlo Scarpa il veneziano", World Architecture, 2, pp. 99-105.
M. BRAWNE, Il museo oggi, Milan.
L. MAGAGNATO, E. RITTER, "Castelvecchio. L'agencement moderne d'un musée ancien", L'Oeil, 121, pp. 54-57 and 68.
P.C. SANTINI, "Il restauro di Castelvecchio a Verona", Comunità, 126, pp. 70-78.

1966
P.C. SANTINI, "Progetto per una casa a Ronco di Carimate", Ottagono, 2, pp. 86-89.

1967
S. Los, Carlo Scarpa architetto poeta,
Venice.
G. MAZZOTTI (ed.), Arturo Martini, exhibition catalogue, Treviso.
B. ZEVI, "L'Italia all'Expò universale 1967", L'architettura-c.s., 141, pp. 142-146.
ed. "Il padiglione italiano all'Expò '67 di Montreal", L'architettura-c.s., 141, pp. 147-155.

1969
C. DE SETA, Scarpa, Carlo, entry in Dizionario Enciclopedico di Architettura e di Urbanistica, Rome, pp. 429-431.
S. Los, "Zwei Restaurierungen von Carlo Scarpa", Werk, 7, pp. 481-492.
P.C. SANTINI, "Tre progetti per il teatro di Vicenza", Ottagono, 15, pp. 104-111.

1970
Scarpa, Carlo, entry in Enciclopedia Universale, Milan, vol. XIII, p. 447.

1972
AA.VV., Great Drawings from the Collection, exhibition catalogue, London.
M. BRUSATIN, "Carlo Scarpa architetto veneziano", Controspazio, 3-4, pp. 2-85.
P.C. SANTINI, "Architettura per una tomba", Ottagono, 26, pp. 94-97.
I. VERCELLONI, "Sul lago di Zurigo. Una villa ricostruita da un architetto poeta", Casa Vogue, 27, pp. 106-113.

1973
P.C. SANTINI, "Scarpiana", Casabella, 374, pp. 42-47.
ed., "Carlo Scarpa", The Architectural Review, 922, pp. 393-396.
Scarpa, Carlo, entry in Enciclopedia dell'Arte, Milan, p. 606.

1974
S. CANTACUZINO, Carlo Scarpa architetto poeta, exhibition catalogue, London.
P. JOLY, "Scarpa 'L'ornement est un crime'", L'Oeil, 233, pp. 30-34.
N. POZZA (ed.), Carlo Scarpa, exhibition catalogue, Vicenza, pp. 1-16.

1975
A. CHASTEL, "A propos d'une exposition (perdue) de Carlo Scarpa, vénitien", Le Monde, 26-27, June.
P. DUBOY, "Locus Solus, Carlo Scarpa et le cimetiére de S. Vito d'Altivole (1969-1975)", L'architecture d'aujourd'hui, 181, pp. 73-86.
L. MIOTTO-MURET, Carlo Scarpa, exhibition catalogue, Paris.

1976
G.D. ROMANELLI, Ottant'anni di architetture e allestimenti alla Biennale di Venezia, Venice.
I. VERCELLONI, "Un restauro vissuto come felice storia familiare", Casa Vogue, 62.
T. YOKOYAMA, "Carlo Scarpa. Savina Zentner House in Zurich, Switzerland", G.A. Houses, 1, p. 186.

1977
C. SCARPA (ed.), Memoriae Causa, Verona.
"Carlo Scarpa", Space Design, 6.

1979
P. FANCELLI, "Carlo Scarpa, disegni", AR, Ordine degli Architetti di Roma, May-June.
P. PORTOGHESI, "The Brion cemetery by Carlo Scarpa", G.A. – Global Architecture, 50.
B. RADICE, "Un architetto a regola d'arte", Modo, 16, pp. 19-21.
P.C. SANTINI, "Ricordando Carlo Scarpa", Ottagono, 55, pp. 36-43.
G. SCARPA (ed.), Carlo Scarpa per Berni-ni, (e.f.c.).
G. SCARPA (ed.), Carlo Scarpa Venezia 1906 – Sendai 1978. I sette fogli giapponesi.
ed., "Per ricordare Carlo Scarpa: i giardini della Fondazione Querini Stampalia a Venezia, una presenza poetica", Abitare, 172, pp. 76-79.

ed., "Projet pour le musée national Picasso", *L'architecture d'aujord'hui*, 202, pp. 81-84.

"Les années 70 de Carlo Scarpa", *AMC – Architecture Mouvement Continuité*, 50.

1980

R. DUBBINI, "Banque à Verone", *L'architecture d'aujord'hui*, 211, pp. 90-92.

P. DUBOY, "Il reale assoluto", *Gran Bazaar*, 10, pp. 136-143.

P.L. NICOLIN, "L'incompiuta. La banca di Carlo Scarpa a Verona", *Lotus International*, 28, pp. 44-55.

A. RUDI, "Il riordino e l'ampliamento della sede centrale della Banca Popolare di Verona", *Lotus International*, 28, pp. 40-43.

P.C. SANTINI, "L'ultima opera di Carlo Scarpa", *Ottagono*, 59, pp. 20-27.

1981

AA.VV., *Carlo Scarpa. Disegni*, exhibition catalogue, Rome.

AA.VV., "Carlo Scarpa. Frammenti 1926/1978", *Rassegna*, 7.

N. MILLER, "The Legendary Castle", *Progressive Architecture*, 5, pp. 118-123.

S. POLANO, *Scarpa, Carlo*, entry in Enciclopedia Italiana, IV Appendix (1961-1978), Rome, p. 278.

P.C. SANTINI, "Banca Popolare di Verona by Carlo Scarpa", *G.A. Document*, 4, pp. 25-29.

K.J. SCHATTNER, "Carlo Scarpa 1906-78", *Baumeister*, 10, pp. 989-1000.

1982

M. FRASCARI, "Das Wahre und die Erscheinung. Der italienische 'Fassadismus' und Carlo Scarpa", *Daidalos – Berlin Architectural Journal*, 6, pp. 37-46.

M. LAUDANI, G. TAMMEO, "Un'opera inedita di Carlo Scarpa. Casa-studio Scatturin a Venezia", *L'architettura-c.s.*, 4, pp. 259-270.

L. MAGAGNATO (ed.), *Carlo Scarpa a*

Castelvecchio, exhibition catalogue, Milan.

L. MAGAGNATO, "Il museo di Scarpa", *Lotus International*, 35, pp. 75-85.

D. STEWART, "Carlo Scarpa. Casa Ottolenghi. Bardolino, Italy, 1975", *G.A. Houses*, 10, p. 30.

M. TAFURI, "Architettura italiana 1944-1981", in AA.VV., *Storia dell'arte italiana. Il Novecento*, VII, Turin, pp. 523-527.

ed., "Banca Popolare di Verona", *A+U - Architecture and Urbanism*, 137, pp. 37-48.

1983

AA.VV., *Carlo Scarpa et le musée de Verone*, exhibition catalogue, Paris.

E. BRU, "Carlo Scarpa: més que el pas del temps", *Quaderns*, 158, pp. 64-65.

M. BRUSATIN, "La tomba dell'architetto", *Eidos*, 1, pp. 22-23.

E. CHIGGIO (ed.), *Carlo Scarpa: dettaglio d'autore*, Venice.

P. DUBOY (ed.), "Carlo Scarpa. Banca Popolare di Verona Head Offices, Verona, Italy, 1973-81", *G.A. - Global Architecture*, 63.

A. GALLI, "Inedito di Carlo Scarpa: tomba Galli a Nervi, Genova", *L'architettura-c.s.*, 7, pp. 508-513.

N. MILLER, "Banca Popolare in Verona", *Bauwelt*, 13, pp. 502-507.

P.L. NICOLIN, "La sua opera più importante. Carlo Scarpa: cimitero-tomba a San Vito d'Altivole", *Lotus International*, 38, pp. 44-53.

G. RALLI, "Un tocco da maestro", *Casa Vogue*, 140, pp. 298-303.

A. RUDI, "A Udine, un'opera di Carlo Scarpa. I vent'anni di Casa Veritti", *Casa Vogue*, 139, pp. 180-197.

F. SEMI, "La storia di un progetto. Masieri Memorial a Venezia", *Gran Bazaar*, 9-10, pp. 180-185.

G. ZAMBONINI, "Process and Theme in the Work of Carlo Scarpa", *Perspecta*, 20, p. 42.

Scarpa, Carlo, entry in Encyclopedia of

Architecture, vol. VI, New York, pp. 672-673.

1984

AA.VV., *Carlo Scarpa. Il progetto per Santa Caterina a Treviso*, exhibition catalogue, Treviso.

F. BERNARDI, "Fra Treviso e Asolo. La Gipsoteca canoviana di Possagno: Carlo Scarpa e l'ineffabilità del vuoto", *Fascicolo*, 18, pp. 2-5.

M. BOTTERO, "Il fenomeno Scarpa", *Abitare*, 229, p. 86.

M.A. CRIPPA, *Carlo Scarpa*, Milan.

F. DAL CO, *Carlo Scarpa il mestiere dell'architetto*, in D. ROSAND (ed.), *Interpretazioni veneziane. Studi di storia dell'arte in onore di Michelangelo Muraro*, Venice, pp. 481-484.

F. DAL CO, G. MAZZARIOL (ed.), *Carlo Scarpa. The Complete Works*, Milan-London.

P. DUBOIS, "Dio è nel particolare", *Gran Bazaar*, 1-2, pp. 86-87.

F. FONATTI, *Elemente des Bauens bei Carlo Scarpa*, Vienna.

G.K. KOENIG, "Dialogando con l'acqua", *Ottagono*, 73, pp. 18-33.

A.F. MARCIANO (ed.), *Carlo Scarpa*, Bologna.

G.D. ROMANELLI, *Museo Correr*, Milan.

P.C. SANTINI, *L'impiego del cemento nei restauri di un maestro: omaggio a Carlo Scarpa*, in G. CARBONARA (ed.), *Restauro e cemento in architettura 2*, Rome, pp. 78-91.

P.C. SANTINI, "Costruire con l'acqua", *Ottagono*, 73, pp. 34-41.

1985

G. CONTESSI, "Il museo Revoltella di Trieste. Uno Scarpa inedito", *Casabella*, 512, pp. 42-43.

S. LOS (ed.), *Verum Ipsum Factum. Il progetto di Carlo Scarpa per l'ingresso dell'Istituto Universitario di Architettura di Venezia*, Venice.

G. NEPI SCIRÈ,, F. VALCANOVER, *Gallerie dell'Accademia di Venezia*, Milan.

L. POLLIFRONE, "Arredare secondo Carlo Scarpa", *Casa Vogue*, 166.

A. RUDI, "La sede storica: dal progetto alla realizzazione", in P. BRU-GNOLI (ed.), Testimonianze di 2000 anni di storia urbana negli edifici centrali della Banca Popolare di Verona, Verona, pp. 155-198.

F. TENTORI, "Un nuovo monumento di C. Scarpa e A. Rudi per Verona", in P. BRUGNOLI (ed.), Testimonianze di 2000 anni di storia urbana negli edifici centrali della Banca Popolare di Verona, Verona, pp. 213-231.

ed.,"La Ca' d'Oro de Nouveau", Connaissance des Arts, October, pp. 72-75.

1986

A. ESPOSITO, L. POLLIFRONE, "Scarpa e Venezia", Domus, 678, pp. IX-XII.

V. MAGNAGO LAMPUGNANI, Carlo Scarpa Architektur, Stuttgart.

G. MAZZARIOL (ed.), Banca Popolare di Gemona. Luciano Gemin architetto, Treviso.

M. MURARO, Civiltà delle ville venete, Udine, pp. 490-495.

ed., "Tre giardini. Querini Stampalia (Venezia)", Abitare, 242, pp. 13-16.

Angelo Masieri Architetto. Casa Giacomuzzi Udine 1949, Udine.

"Carlo Scarpa", Les cahiers de la recherche architecturale, 19.

1987

C. DE SETA, Carlo Scarpa, l'utopia inattuale della forma, in Architetti Italiani del Novecento, Bari.

A. DI LIETO, "Alcune note sui materiali del restauro di Scarpa a Castelvecchio", Civiltà veronese, 7, pp. 75-82.

M. FRASCARI, "The Body and Architecture in the Drawings of Carlo Scarpa", Res, 14, pp. 123-142.

C. HOH-SLODCZYK, Carlo Scarpa und das Museum, Berlin.

G. MAZZARIOL, "Da Carlo Scarpa: due porte, l'ombra, la luce", Venezia Arti. Bollettino del Dipartimento di Storia e Critica delle Arti dell'Università di Venezia, pp. 73-81.

S. POLANO, "Frammenti siciliani, Carlo Scarpa e Palazzo Abatellis", Lotus International, 53, pp. 108-127.

S. POLANO, M. MULAZZANI, "Forgotten Works of Carlo Scarpa (1)", A+U - Architecture and Urbanism, 204, pp. 83-94.

ed., "Oasi in laguna", Ville e Giardini, December, pp. 50-55.

1988

B. ALBERTINI, S. BAGNOLI, Scarpa. L'architettura in dettaglio, Milan.

A. DONAGGIO, "Biennale di Venezia, un secolo di storia", Art Dossier, 26.

M. GARBERI, A. PIVA (ed.), L'opera d'arte e lo spazio architettonico. Museografia e museologia, Milan, pp. 49-58.

R. JACQUES, "Scarpa masterclass", Building Design, January.

M. MULAZZANI, I padiglioni della Biennale, Venezia 1887-1988, Milan.

M. MULAZZANI, "La storia del Padiglione Italia", Casabella, 551, pp. 10-14.

S. POLANO, Mostrare. L'allestimento in Italia dagli anni Venti agli anni Ottanta, Milan.

T. SAMMARTINI, "Carlo Scarpa a Edimburgo", Parametro, pp. 163-164.

G. TOLMEIN, "Taufrisch: ein Haus in den Jahren", Hauser, 1, pp. 46-53.

ed., "Carlo Scarpa. Selected Drawings", G.A. Document, 21.

1989

M. BOTTERO, "Carlo Scarpa: lo spazio poetico del Cimitero Brion", Abitare, 272, pp. 208-211.

P. DUBOIS, P. NOEVER (ed.), Carlo Scarpa Die Andere Stadt, Vienna.

P. MORELLO, Palazzo Abatellis, Treviso.

S. POLANO, Carlo Scarpa: Palazzo Abatellis, Milan.

C. SCARPA, "Può l'architettura essere poesia?", Casabella, 526, pp. 25-26.

G. SCARPINI (ed.), "Il gusto veneto: il caso Vicenza", Abitare, 272, pp. 172-186.

1990

G. PIETROPOLI, "L'invitation au voyage", Spazio e Società, April-June, pp. 90-97.

ed., "Ein schlichtes Palazzetto wurde zur Passion", Hauser, 4, pp. 14-25.

Casa Balboni, Demeures secrètes de Venise, Paris.

1991

M. BAROVIER (ed.), Carlo Scarpa. I vetri di Murano. 1927-1947, Venice.

S. MARINELLI, Castelvecchio a Verona, Milan.

R. MURPHY, Carlo Scarpa e Castelvecchio, Venice.

1992

B. ALBERTINI, S. BAGNOLI, Scarpa. I musei e le esposizioni, Milan.

M. COVI, "Tendenze dagli anni '80 ai primi '90", in S. POLANO, L. SEMERANI (ed.), Friuli Venezia Giulia. Guida all'architettura contemporanea, Venice, pp. 180-191.

R. MASIERO, Museo Revoltella. Leggendo il progetto di Carlo Scarpa, catalogue.

R. MASIERO, "Un'architettura differita: il Museo Revoltella di Carlo Scarpa", Casabella, 588, pp. 38-39.

F. TENTORI, "Friuli: anni '50", in S. POLANO, L. SEMERANI (ed.), Friuli Venezia Giulia. Guida all'architettura contemporanea, Venice, pp. 146-153.

1993

F. DAL CO, "La maturità di Carlo Scarpa", Piranesi, 3, vol. 2, pp. 10-32.

G. MORELLI, "Estrarre il vuoto dal vero", Piranesi, 3, vol. 2, pp. 38-43.

G. TOMMASI, "Quattro progetti per Villa Ottolenghi", Piranesi, 3, vol. 2, pp. 33-37.

1994

R. BORGHI, "Prova d'autore", Ville e Giardini, 295, September, pp. 21-27.

A. DE ECCHER, G. DEL ZOTTO, Venezia e il Veneto, l'opera di Carlo Scarpa, Milan.

S. LOS, Carlo Scarpa, Cologne.

Index of names and places

The **bold** faced names and numbers refer to the progressive numbers of the files.